THE WURMBRAND LETTERS

To my beloved wife, Binzea, who has shared every part of the trials, joys and hopes described in this "book of letters."

RICHARD WURMBRAND

THE
WURMBRAND
LETTERS

CROSS PUBLICATIONS, INC.
Pomona, California

Illustrated by

THE REV. THOMAS E. MAILS

© CROSS PUBLICATIONS, INC.
Pomona, California
1967

Printed in the United States of America

TABLE OF CONTENTS

WHY I WRITE THIS BOOK

Every freedom-loving man has two fatherlands; his own and America. Today, America is the hope of every enslaved man, because it is the last bastion of freedom in the world. Only America has the power and spiritual resources to stand as a barrier between militant Communism and the peoples of the world. It is the repository of the hopes of millions of people around the world. It is the last "dike" holding back the rampaging flood-waters of militant Communism. If it crumples, there is no other dike; no other dam; no other line of defense to fall back upon. America is the last hope of millions of enslaved peoples. They look to it as their second fatherland. In it lies their hopes and prayers. I have seen fellow-prisoners in Communist prisons beaten, tortured, with fifty pounds of chains on their legs — praying for America . . . that the dike will not crumple; that it will remain free. I, too, have shared this hope and prayer with my fellow-prisoners. Now I share a great concern for America. This gives me the right and duty to speak. For me and for millions of enslaved around the world America is our last resort.

A native of Rumania, I have been an eye-witness to my "first" fatherland's betrayal, overthrow and fall to Communism. It has not been through sheer, brute, military force of the Soviets but also through a subtle and infinitely clever betrayal from within which paved the way for the final physical take over. I wept when I saw it happen before my eyes. Now that I have come to America, I have been astonished beyond words and deeply grieved as I see the same symptoms, the same step-by-step betrayal which overthrew my first fatherland. It is like a nightmare which I have lived through, happening again . . . coming back a second time. I spoke out without counting the cost when I eye-witnessed my first fatherland, Rumania, being betrayed. I will not now remain silent as I see the same symptoms, the same tragedy beginning to happen again to my second fatherland, America.

In Communist prisons, one thing that helped me survive, when so many died all around me, was the hope that one day I would be free and would be able to warn the western world about the Communist menace. This I have tried to do in my contacts with some of your western church leaders. But I met their enmity, their indifference . . . and even their complicity with the Communists. Therefore, I appeal to you, the rank and file Christians.

I have spoken personally and corresponded with many of your church leaders in the West. I have poured forth my heart to them. I have warned them of the very things I witnessed personally before and urged them to beware. I have challenged them to a course of action which can prevent America from falling to the fate of my homeland. I publish in this book excerpts of my letters to them.

I have not been heeded. My warnings have been ignored. I have been looked upon as an embarrassment to those I warned and who have a responsibility to the people they lead. They have not only turned aside my pleadings with them to beware the snare into which they lead their people, but some have actively worked to silence my voice. Yet, Communist torturers could not silence me with their hot irons and knives and I will not be silenced now. I owe it to my second fatherland, to the millions of Americans who do not see their betrayal taking place. I owe it to the millions around the earth — in Communist prisons, in slave-labor camps, in Communist cities where the air of oppression is crushing — who look to America as their hope.

"We will put the Red Flag upon the White House in Washington, and if necessary, we will fill the Pacific Ocean with blood to attain this aim." This is the warning of the Red Guard, which, under Mao-Tse-Tung controls every fourth man in the world.

This alone should be enough to alert Americans. Before my country of Rumania was taken over by Communism, we never had even this much warning.

Some of the political and religious leaders of America silence public opinion, telling us that the Chinese have no means to fulfill their avowed aims. It is no secret that Marx, Lenin and after them, every major Communist leader has declared the triumph of Communism over the globe as being their goal which they will pursue to the end. Only a few months ago, Breshnev and Kosygin declared that the differences between them and the Chinese are of minor importance and that Russian and Chinese Communists can very well unite in their fight. The differences between the Russian and Chinese Communist leaderships are merely tactical and strategic differences, not differences in their aims.

Today, all the Communists of the world have America as their principal target. It is the last and only bastion of defense left. If it falls the globe is theirs.

Specialists in rockets, missiles and nuclear weapons can assure us that the Chinese will not have the power to launch an offensive for another ten or fifteen years. This does not ease the concern of any conscientious man for it means his children who now play with toys on the carpet will face this fate. They will know the horror of nuclear war.

"But America can retaliate with its missiles! Isn't this thought enough to stop them?" This is the oft-repeated defense to such danger. The Communists have already foreseen this and Mao-Tse-Tung has said, "I am not afraid if 300,000,000 Chinese will die in a nuclear war. Another 300,000,000 will remain, but imperialism will be destroyed." This is the exact concept of Lenin.

Maxim Gorki, the great Russian writer, tells us in his book, *Remembrances About Lenin,* that when he reproached Lenin about the mass killing in the Revolution, Lenin laughed and said, "You can't make omelets without breaking eggshells and you can't cut wood without making chips fly." For Lenin the life of a man was worth as much as a chip or an eggshell. As a consequence of his materialistic philosophy he could make no difference between a man and a material object. In his heart there was no compassion for the pain of man, for the trouble of his soul, for the tears of mothers, widows or orphans.

Leninists think like Lenin. In this respect there is no difference between Chinese, Russian or American Communists. The only difference is that the Chinese Communists think an offensive war should be begun immediately. The others wish to begin the war later. First, they say, the Americans should be made to fall asleep and be attacked only when they are very sure that nobody threatens them, that peaceful co-existence is assured. Remember Pearl Harbor, when you were also attacked by a people with whom you were at peace.

The Chinese say attack now. The Russian Communists ask for the intermediate step of lulling Americans to sleep — to undermine the will to resist — to chip away their resistance. This is the difference between Chinese and Russian Communism.

What the Chinese Communist leadership thinks, we have seen above. Now listen to the Russian. I quote from Manuilski, one of their great strategists of the Communist world revolution:

"War to the hilt between Communism and capitalism is inevitable. Today, of course, we are not strong enough to attack. Our time will come in twenty or thirty years. The bourgeoisie will have to be put to sleep, so we will begin by launching the most spectacular peace movement on record. There will be electrifying overtures and unheard of concessions. The capitalist countries, stupid and decadent, will rejoice to cooperate in their own destruction. They will leap at another chance to be friends. As soon as their guard is down, we shall smash them with our clenched fist."

WHAT A COMMUNIST TAKE OVER IS LIKE

I have been an eye-witness to the Communist take over of my homeland. I have lived under Communism. I can assure you it is not simply "changing one social order for another." It is not simply a "different approach to economic problems." A take over by Communism is the total destruction of civilization as we know it and everything we hold dear. It is a violent destruction of all values, the ferocity of which you cannot imagine. I have seen it happen with my eyes.

I can tell you firsthand the future which men are planning now for America and your little "Mary" or your little "Billy" who now play on the carpet before your eyes.

It is said that one out of five of our people of Rumania has passed through Communist prisons. In America, where religion is stronger and capitalism flourishes and you have such independent, free people, it will be a much greater number. I have seen prisons packed with prisoners. The youngest was 9, the oldest 92. I have seen Christian children of 13 with their teeth kicked out and their bones broken, lying in cells in agony. I have seen children beaten to death before the eyes of their parents because these were Christians. The horrible sounds of cells full of young children crying in the dark for their mothers and fathers can never be told. I have heard this many, many nights all night long. This is a Communist take over. It is not a "changing of social systems," but a bloody purge which reaches out to touch almost every family of a country. In our land, almost every family had a loved one imprisoned, beaten, tortured or killed.

Recently in Red China, Catholic priests were buried alive. We have news that the Red Guard which beat men publicly on the streets has gone into the jails and there, out of sight, has cut off the ears, tongues and legs of Christian prisoners. A renowned evangelical writer who has been imprisoned for twelve years, suffered this fate.

If the Communists come to power in America, this will be your fate and the fate of your children. It will touch every family as it did with us in Rumania. In the pages which follow, you will read of many proofs from Communist sources about the anti-Christian terror now reigning in the Communist countries. Just now, mass-arrests of Christians are happening across Russia. Some of those arrested have died as a result of the tortures. This is in Russia. Today! There has never existed one Communist country in which Christians have not been jailed, unspeakably tortured and killed. Is America — the big target — going to be any different? Remember, this isn't research, study or hypothetical dreaming. I have seen it happen. This is the "paradise" and the "new social order" which the Communists prepare for America.

Read the books of Marx and Lenin and you will see that they will never be satisfied with less than world revolution. The whole world must be under their domination. Some say they are becoming more "practical" and "realistic" and not so doctrinaire. This is the "intermediate" step to lull America to sleep.

When this paradise comes, your church will be closed, your barbershop, your tailorshop, your private business will be stopped and your property will be taken away. Sheep, cattle and all land have been taken from our farmers. Our farmers have to work as slaves on their former farms receiving in exchange a salary of $20 to $30 a month. Our farmers have little bread and no meat and no fruit.

The Russian Communists scoff at their Chinese comrades because they have forbidden Shakespeare and Beethoven. They scoff about this loudly but they do the same thing. In no bookshop in Moscow or in Bucharest can one find the books of Plato, of Kant, of Spinoza. They have taken out the masterpieces of human culture. In science, our universe is called the Einsteinian Universe because Einstein discovered its last laws. The book of Einstein, *How I See the World,* is forbidden in Russia, Rumania and other Communist lands because it is a book which draws religious conclusions from science. If Communism triumphs in America not only will religion be abolished and destroyed, but all literature and the whole of culture will come under Communist censorship.

The whole of life will be paralyzed. I have seen even the following: a young Christian has a girl friend. The girl was called by the Communist youth organization and told she must choose another boy friend. The one whom she now has is the son of a "counter-revolutionary" Christian. I have seen the secret police dictate boy friends, girl friends, husbands, wives. And woe to any who does not obey!

After many years every vestige of freedom and individuality will vanish. I have led a secret missionary work in the Russian Army for several years. One of the most dramatic moments of my life was when I met the first Russian officer. He told me that he was an engineer. When I asked him if he believed in God I was prepared for an answer that, "yes," he believed in God or "no," he did not. Instead, he lifted to me eyes that were filled with a void — a lack of understanding and said, "We have no such order to believe in a God." He was a robot, believing what the leaders told him to believe. He was the product of years of Communist indoctrination. Your future generations will be as this officer if you are lulled into the fatal sleep. Can you afford to be?

To be tortured was not the worst thing. Christian children were obliged to denounce their parents, revealing whether their parents had said a word against Communism or for God. Listen to Chinese radio broadcasts and you will hear children who have demanded the death sentence for the parents proclaimed as heroes!

I have seen a Christian whose toes were all cut off in order to make him denounce his brethren. Christians have been kept on ice for many hours, losing their feet to frostbite. In the prison of Fagaras, Christians have been forced to kneel on broken nut shells for hours with their hands lifted up. Try to do it yourself for thirty minutes! You cannot, but it will be good for you, for you will know the "social change" which Communism will bring. You will know what will happen to your children whom you love so ardently.

I have seen men beaten at the bottom of the feet until the flesh was torn off. The next day they were beaten as hard as before, but this time there was no flesh left. This has happened to me. Words are not adequate to say what pain this is. The next time you kiss the feet of your little babies, remember that, if you sleep the fatal sleep, those feet may be beaten in such a manner.

Don't accept the lulling words that Communism is just another "social philosophy." As one who has experienced it for many years, I can assure you it is not a philosophy. It is organized crime.

THE COMMUNIST STRATEGY TODAY

The immediate strategy of the Communists this minute is not to launch a missile raid. It is not to overthrow militarily, except where they have the force, such as in Vietnam. There is an intermediate step first. It is this step they all — with the exception of Red China which wants immediate war — are concentrating on. Every facet of their power is directed to this step. Their diplomatic fronts, their "culture-exchange fronts," their "religious fronts" — all are weapons used to achieve this intermediate step. And that step is to lull America to sleep, to cause her not to think about the Communist menace, to forget, not to take the Communist menace seriously, to believe there are means to co-exist peacefully. When this intermediate step is reached — when America sleeps — then Communism will attack, and this tragic fate which I saw befall my homeland will befall yours. The nightmare of horrors I have seen fall upon our children will fall upon yours.

In the biography of Stalin, we find the following incident: Once Lenin, Trotsky, Stalin and other Communist leaders went together on a hunting party. There, during an evening after the hunting, Lenin asked his comrades, "What is the greatest pleasure?" One said, "Wine." Another said, "Women." And still another said, "Power." Stalin alone was quiet, not speaking. Lenin insisted that he should say what he too considered the greatest pleasure. After some hesitation he answered: "You don't know what pleasure is. Pleasure is to hate a man from all your heart, but make him believe you are his friend. And when he believes in you the most, when he rests his weary head on your shoulders, then to plunge a knife into his back. There is no greater joy than this." The entire life of Stalin and his successors is proof this "pleasure" has permeated every activity of Communism. The strategy of Communism is to make the adversary fall asleep and then plunge the knife in his back. This happened to us. Remember Pearl Harbor and don't be lulled to sleep by the illusion of peaceful co-existence!

Don't forget that not long ago America believed Mao-Tse-Tung and Fidel Castro to be nothing but agricultural reformers. Castro was called "the George Washington of Cuba." Church leaders assured America that Fidel Castro was not a Communist. They believed his word. He hid the fact he was a Communist until he came to power, and men believed him, were duped by him and allowed him to succeed. Then, and only then, Castro removed his mask and a sleeping America awoke to find itself ninety miles from Communism. Deceit has and always will be the most powerful tool the Communists use. They never run out of gullible people who believe them.

Communism is preparing the systematic destruction of Christian civilization and the introduction of their system of atheistic slavery over all the world. America is the last roadblock. Is it not logical that all of Communism's "guns," tools, deceit, duplicity and treachery are turned on America?

And my impression is that beleaguered America is now being lured into a fatal sleep by the swan song of a "changed" Communism and by church leaders who close the eyes of America so it will not see the approaching Communist menace. Worse still, many of the leaders of the Church are collaborating with the Communists in attaining their goal. Some of them are nothing else but agents of Communism in disguise.

With Church leaders I have been unsuccessful. Now I take my appeal and warning to the rank and file Christian. Jesus also appealed to the people against the religious leaders whose wrong attitude paved the way for the destruction of Jerusalem.

I had the curiosity to peruse the periodicals of the Russian Orthodox Church published before 1917 — the year the Communists took over Russia.

One year before the Communists came to power in Russia, the leadership of the Orthodox Church did not believe Communism to be even a distant menace. No earnest warning against it appears in even one of their periodicals even a few months before the take over! The church leaders did not strike the alarm bell. The Christians were not told of it by their leaders. They were sleeping. The punishment for sleeping has been horrible. Tens of thousands of priests, pastors, and millions of Christians have perished by torture, execution and planned starvation. The Russian General Berman, boasted before me that he had thrown priests into the Black Sea, shouting to the drowning, "May God rescue you."

I examined the periodicals of Christian Missions in China, published one year before the Communists came to power. There was scarcely any mention of the menace of Communism or that it might possibly take over China. The menace was not seen and the Christians slept, lulled to sleep by Christian leaders who did not see and who did not warn — even one year before the nightmare engulfed China!

Can we not see the lessons from history? Christian leaders did not sound the alarm even though the foe was at the door. They lulled the people to sleep and then the nightmare came. The same is happening again, only this time in the last bastion of freedom, the last line of defense, America. Some of our Christian leaders do not warn you and do not sound the alarm. Instead they allow the wolf to come to the sleeping lambs.

In my own fatherland, no one believed, even one year before the take over that Communists would ever rule. When they came to power in Rumania, the number of members of the Communist party was only ten thousand in a country of 18,000,000. We considered Communism as a joke.

During the war, I spoke with Church leaders in my homeland and told them, "Let us prepare for the possibility that the Russians will invade our country and impose Communism on us! Let us create secret Bible supplies! Let us print Christian literature disproving atheism and hide it until such time! Let us ordain pastors who will not reveal themselves as pastors now, but be prepared for the time when the known pastors will be put in prison!"

I was considered to be a madman. The church leaders were very sure it was not a menace. They said, "Surely the Communists are no longer as they were in the years of the Russian revolution. They have mellowed. They have changed. They will be civilized and we will be able to be good neighbors with them." Church leaders lived under these illusions as they do today. They did not prepare themselves or their flocks for the victory of Communism which very soon became a fact.

I see happening in America now the same things which happened before in the countries which are now under Communist rule. Why is it that some of the political and religious leaders don't fulfill their duty to alert America to the Communist menace? Why, instead, do they lull America to sleep? We who come from behind the Iron Curtain and who have seen this all happen before have the answer to these questions.

In Rumania the Minister of Interior Affairs, Ghelmegeanu, was the one who, in Nazi times, led the anti-Communist fight. All the time he was actually a member of the Communists. The Rumanian secret police reported to him about the Communist conspiracy. He, the Minister of Interior Affairs of the anti-Communist government, passed these reports directly to the hands of the secret Communist leadership. Now, all the former political leaders in Rumania have been put in prison. However, this man has been greatly honored by the Communists!

Professor Constantinescu-Tashi was a professor of Theology in the Orthodox seminary. He taught young men to be priests. These young men did not know that he was secretly a member of the Communist party. When the Communists came to power, this professor became head of the Communist department of cults. His job was to uproot religion and destroy the very young men he had prepared as priests. By his signature, thousands have been put in prison and tortured. Some of them, the very young men he taught to be ministers, were the victims.

The former Orthodox priests, Patrashcoiu and Riosheanu, are now colonels of the Communist secret police. They had been leading priests of the Orthodox Church. When the Communists came to power, they shaved off their beards, removed their clerical robes and dressed in the uniforms of the secret police. They personally arrested and tortured the Christians they had "led" for so many years.

I could give many such other cases, with names and facts.

The secretary of the Protestant seminary of Cluj, Bende, now declares openly that he has long been a member of the Communist party and that they had sent him to work in the Theological seminary in order secretly to propagate Communism among the students.

We, who have seen these things with our eyes, have the strong opinion that the American Communists have their members in church councils, in the committees of different denominations and in the political institutions of America.

Imagine the feelings of Rumanian Christians who were arrested in the night, hauled before the secret police and saw there, standing before them in the uniform of the secret police, their former priest who had taken their confessions! Now this "priest" has a whip in his hands, and beats and tortures them. When the Christians ask, "How can you beat me?" the secret police laughs saying, "You idiot, you dupe, you believed us. We knew how to deceive you."

I have seen this very incident happen. Others, after torture, have told me of their shock and disbelief. But it happened . . . and it can surely happen again.

Your children may have the same experience. Some church leaders are surely playing the same role now, which church leaders played in our country. Your children may be beaten by those who have given them Holy Communion, by those who now pose as world-wide known church leaders.

A man named Tibacu was one of the top men of the anti-Communist secret police in the province of Bessarabia. Later it was discovered that all the time he had been a leader of the Communists. A man named Banciulescu was the leader of the anti-Communist police of Bucharest. He knew all the active anti-Communist police who worked under him. When the Communists took over it was revealed that all along he was with the Communists. You will have such surprises in America, too.

I am very well aware that those are rare cases. I don't believe that many of your church leaders are simply Communists in disguise and conscious agents of Communism. Most of them are simply duped and have a criminal ignorance of facts. Ignorance is not an excuse when so much is at stake. A man who is ignorant in questions of war should not become a general. He can't excuse the fact that his army was brought to defeat and destroyed because he did not know his enemy. And a man who is ignorant of the satanic spiritual forces embodied in atheistic Communism has no right to be a leader in spiritual matters. When the battle is finished in tragedy — as it is in Rumania — he cannot say, "I didn't know, I was duped." Most of your great religious leaders are simply duped and deceived. As honest men, they believe Communist assertions that they can co-exist. But some world church leaders play the same ugly role of betrayal which the priests whose names I gave have played in our country.

I met with one of the greatest personalities of Christian life in the West.

I told him to his face that I considered him to be a traitor. Now, what would you do if I would enter your office and call you a traitor? If you are not a traitor, you would probably tell me to get out of your office at once. If you are a very meek Christian, you would control your natural wrath, and if there is no treason in your heart, you would explain to me in humble words that I am mistaken to call you a traitor. If you reproach a woman of adultery and she is innocent, she will either get upset or she will explain to you that you have been mistaken to accuse her. If, instead, she falls on her knees and cries forth, "Let us pray," it is an acknowledgment of the adultery. When I told this great church leader that, in my opinion, he is a traitor, he fell in my arms and said, "Let us pray." He knew that he was a traitor. You Americans have such church leaders as we have had and they lead you to the red pastures, not to the green ones.

Love and seduction both use the same vocabulary — the same words — the same phraseology. If I wish to marry a girl, I tell her, "I love you." And if I wish to have a girl just for a night and then throw her away like a dirty rag, I tell her also, "I love you." How vital and urgent it is for a girl to be wise and to distinguish and to see what is behind the words of love! So the Communist propaganda uses beautiful words; the same words which real lovers of humanity use. They use also the words of freedom, of democracy, of religion — all kinds of beautiful words and by this they deceive sincere Christian leaders and laymen who cannot distinguish between love and seduction.

Never will Americans be able to understand how much Communists lie and deceive until they experience it firsthand, which I pray will never happen. Their father is the devil who is the father of lies.

For example, for fourteen years of prison, our food was horribly bad. Prisoners were forced to eat their own excrements and to drink urine. At another time, we ate cabbage with unwashed intestines. This is what we had for fourteen years . . . except on one wonderful day. On that day we had exceptionally good food. It was a roast beef with noodle soup and mashed potatoes. Following this was fruit cake. We shabby prisoners wondered what had happened. Later we found out. A delegation of leftist women organizations from Great Britain, America and the Scandinavian lands had come to visit our country and they asked to visit a prison, too. They were brought to the prison where I was at the time imprisoned. There, they were shown some cells of prisoners which were beautiful with carpets, curtains, furniture — totally unlike our real cells, which were sometimes filled with hungry rats to keep us from sleeping and where we lay on hardwood slabs. In the faked cells, the ladies from the free world were shown "prisoners" — fat, happy, well-fed and well-dressed. They were members of the secret police posing as prisoners! But the ladies were shrewd. They said, "Oh, we will not allow ourselves to be duped by the Communists. We wish to see the kitchen. We wish to see the food which the prisoners eat." They were promptly taken to the "kitchen" and saw the food: the roast beef, the noodles, the mashed potatoes, the fruit cakes. This convinced them. They went back to their homelands and reported what fine food the Communists served in their prisons. Please don't ask me what we ate the next day, the next month and the next year !

The Communists are masters at such deception and your leaders fall for it just as these women did. They come to our lands and "see" freedom of religion. They "see" so-called "pastors" preaching the Gospel. They come back to America praising freedom of religion because they have "seen" such "open, free churches." You have all heard or read of such "eye-witness" reports from tourists and visiting ministers.

As a Christian must know God, so he must know the devil and all his devices. If he doesn't know them, he will be his victim. If he doesn't know the devil and his devices, he can't be a good church leader. Most of your top church officials are sincere men ignoring the devil's devices, but it is a criminal ignorance. Some, I am convinced, are themselves Communists.

The head of one of America's leading denominations has written a circular letter in which, after complimenting me for having been fourteen years in prison for the Gospel's sake and assuring everybody that he highly esteems me for the cross I have borne, he urged them to close their doors and silence me. Other leaders rejected my warning, though it is based on uncontrovertible evidence. Therefore, I appeal to you rank and file Christians and pastors. Pass over their heads and defend yourselves and your country against the fatal menace which they say does not exist. Defend the churches! Defend your Bibles! Defend your children's future! Defend your free country which is "everyman's second homeland!" There is no hope from many of your church leaders. They are totally duped.

Many of them speak in your name without any right. Do they speak for you when they wine and dine Communist agents from behind the Iron Curtain while Christian martyrs starve? Do they speak for you when they kiss Communist "bishops" who are personally responsible for the murdering of many Christians? Do they speak for you when they work together with the paid agents of the Russian secret police? Do you give your name to such use?

Most American Christians are not even aware of what is happening and what is done in their name and with their money. They do not agree at all. In the short time I have been in America I have preached evening after evening, after which we have question and answer sessions. Never has anyone spoken to defend the world and national church organizations and their leaders who do this. The leaders of these groups are self-appointed, but purport to speak in the name of American Christianity. It is a disgrace to every American Christian.

One can easily recognize an American church leader to be Moscow's mouthpiece, even when he disguises himself, if you apply the following test: When he protests against racial discrimination in the United States, South Africa and Rhodesia, does he condemn also the uprooting of the Tibetan people by Red China, does he condemn anti-Semitism in the Communist countries? When he protests apartheid against negroes in Africa, does he also speak out against apartheid regarding white men in Communist countries, where one has to suffer if he is a Christian? When he speaks against the Americans fighting in Vietnam, does he speak also against the North Vietnamese aggression in South Vietnam? Does he speak against the crushing of the Hungarian revolution by the Russians? When he asks for the admission of Red China in the UN, does he speak out also against the mass-killing of men in Red China? Does he ask that the Communist countries should respect the charter of the UN, which obliges them to safeguard political and religious liberties? When he speaks about peaceful dialogue with the Marxists, ask him how it is with the victims of the Marxists, with the thousands of Christian martyrs in the Communist camp! Does he care for these martyrs? Does he ask from the Marxists with whom he discusses a protest against the torturing and killing of his Christian brethren in the Communist camp? He says that he is a leader of the Church of Christ. Jesus commanded: "Go and teach all the nations." What missionary activity in Communist countries does your church leader organize? If he is a church leader, he is supposed to be in communion of saints. He must be in communion with St. Mary Magdalene who took a pound of ointment of spikenard, and anointed the feet of Jesus. Do you know that he has given up ornaments and costly articles and jewels in his and his family's lives, all luxury and every waste, to bring them to the mystical body of Christ, the Church, which is tortured in Communist lands even now? Does he oppose the official delegates of the Eastern churches who come to the West and praise the liberties of Communism?

I wish you to think logically with me about the most interesting situation which follows:

Of the thousands of Communist officials — staffs of embassies, sports groups, etc., coming to the West, every professional category has had its defectors to freedom. Communist newspapermen, athletes, diplomats, artists, ballet dancers, even officers of the secret police have defected to the West. Every professional category has had its defectors. Every category except one: the so-called religious leaders who come to the World Council of Churches or to the National Council of Churches. Not one of them has ever defected. Every other category has had at least one defector — EVEN THE SECRET POLICE. Why is it that the anti-religious Communists can count on their "religious leaders" even more than they can count on their own secret police? Why are religious leaders more trustworthy and loyal to Communism than even the secret police? I leave it to the reader to draw the conclusions from this undeniable fact.

We, who come from Communist lands, understand why none of the so-called "religious leaders" have defected while some from every other category have. Why should Patriarch Justinian of Rumania defect? He has been with the Communists long before they came to power. He is one of the chief architects of the brutal Communist take over and the subsequent torture and killing of Christians. Why should he defect? Why should the Patriarch-Deputy Tonescu defect? He has been with the Communists long before they came to power. When Communists took over, at once we, who thought him to be a real priest, were shocked to see him put the hammer and sickle on his priestly robe. He demanded we all call him "Comrade Bishop."

The same thing has happened in Russia and other Communist lands.

Secondly, the religious "leaders" of the Communist lands are unspeakably rich for the conditions existing there. The anti-religious newspapers of Russia have published that their metropolitans and patriarchs have bank accounts which, in some instances, amount to 300,000 rubles, which is a fantastic sum for Russia. You will find no Russian who has such a sum of money — or even a tenth this amount. Why should they defect? Why should they not go back to an anti-religious regime which keeps in utter poverty its citizens, but gives great sums of money to "bishops," "patriarchs" and "religious leaders" who beautifully play the role of deceiving the West and infiltrate the church bodies of the West. Again, why should they defect? None ever have.

No religious leader who comes with an official delegation from the Communist lands is entirely reliable.

Let us take the case of a Yugoslav official church representative who came to the West and spoke at a church meeting which was held in Europe. He praised the religious liberty in Yugoslavia, which is only a partial liberty, and that of only recent origin. Tito gives no liberty to his own Communist comrades. Djilas, a Communist like Tito who dared to express political opinions very slightly different from those of Tito, has been imprisoned for years. Recently Mihalov and five of his comrades have been put in prison for criticizing Tito from a Socialist point of view. Now, if Tito does now allow even the slightest political contradiction from fellow Communists, who can believe that he will allow the full Gospel, that he will allow meaningful spreading of Christianity "to every creature" which is just on the opposite extreme of Communism?

Communism asserts that there is no God and no Christ. Christianity means love toward the Creator and toward the Savior. Communism is the religion of hatred; Christianity is the religion of love. Communism says that man is only matter and that, when he dies, he becomes salt and mineral. Christianity says that man is first of all spirit, and that he lives eternally and has to prepare himself for this eternal life. Communism denies the Holy Scriptures and mocks them. For Christians, the Holy Scriptures are the words of God. Who can believe that Tito, who puts in prison Djilas will allow the free, unfettered preaching of the Gospel?

Yes, the "gospel" is preached in thousands of churches in Yugoslavia — Orthodox, Catholic and Protestant churches — but a curtailed, compromised, falsified and distorted gospel; a gospel which does not denounce the greatest crime committed these days in humanity: the crime of poisoning youth and children with atheism. If Christianity does not proclaim its eternal truth, if Christianity does not oppose evil, it is not a Christianity anymore. Only such a falsified Christianity in which Christ cannot be proclaimed King is free in Yugoslavia.

The Bible says, "Woe to those who call the evil good and the good evil," and many Protestant leaders in Communist countries are guilty of this. The Yugoslavian delegates know very well that clergymen and simple Christians of his country have been killed, tortured and jailed by Tito. Until recently they were not permitted to run Sunday schools, to have church meetings, to publish books which would counteract the atheistic poison, that they have no right to prove the Christian truth and to spread it widely. Yet notwithstanding, he calls the evil good and praises the liberties of Communism.

If there is religious liberty in Yugoslavia, we can expect these brethren to tell us when we can hear a religious service on the radio from Yugoslavia. We will also expect information about the kind of Sunday school there, and he should show us the anti-atheistic books published by his denomination.

Wolves come dressed in sheepskins and they lead astray the Western Christians. And Western church leaders, some consciously, some unconsciously, have helped the wolf to enter the fold of the sheep.

As one who has personally passed through this tragic experience, I can predict that on the day you will expect them least, these wolves will drop their sheepskins and show their real faces, and you will see some of your church leaders as obedient servants of Communism, as Communist propagandists, as Communist rulers, as we have in Rumania. And then your children will be tortured by the Communists, just as we have been tortured.

Look again at your Mary, at your Steve, at your George, who are playing now with their toys on the carpet and think what will happen to them when they are 20 or 25 years old if things continue to go as they go now!

In our country, Christians have been stripped naked and have been obliged to crawl on the floor with their hands handcuffed on the back, and on the floor there were hundreds of pieces of splintered glass. Whipped, they had to crawl on this splintered glass until their bodies were torn into ribbons.

In our country, Christians were tied to crosses. Every day the crosses were put on the floor. Hundreds of prisoners were obliged to fulfill their bodily necessities upon the faces and upon the bodies of the crucified ones. Then the crosses were erected for the amusement of the Communists who stood around jeering: "Look at your Christ; how beautiful He is." Imagine your George and your Steve, at the age of 20, put in this condition! Christian girls have been turned over to the lusts of Communist brutes. They have been raped, they have been beaten or they have been tickled shamefully with pig bristles on the sensitive parts nearly unto death, being handcuffed and not having the possibility to defend themselves. This will be the fate of your Mary, or your Esther, if you will not be aware of the menace of Communism in your country and in your churches.

At a recent meeting of churchmen in Europe, all measures were taken that no word should be said against Communism. But God, who is more powerful than all the devices of man, has intervened. The Korean and Chinese delegates have told of atrocities of Communism. They have told the story of 3,000,000 Christians tortured and killed in North Korea alone.

Then one of the great Christian personalities of the West, seeing that the delegates were shocked, said: "We must pray." With this very holy phrase everybody fell on his knees, a prayer was said and the entire issue was immediately forgotten. No one said, "Let us organize a secret evangelistic work behind the Iron Curtain, although the Communists forbid it! Let us help the families of Christian martyrs there! Let us bring into the Communist countries Bibles and other Christian literature to counteract the poison of Communism! And only if we do this, let us pray that this work will be successful." But to say the holy words "let us pray" without drawing the right conclusions from what has been said about the crimes of the Communists means, unconsciously, to help Communists to continue with their crimes, just as they have done it until now.

The reader would be very interested in pictures taken recently at trials of Russian Baptists. The pictures are easily found in Soviet newspapers, and below the pictures the Soviet newspaper gives the "crime" of these Baptists: it is to have taught children about Christ! We possess excerpts of many current Soviet newspapers, giving the names of those sentenced to five or ten years of prison for having spoken to children about Christ.

You, Christian parents of America, are surely very happy about your children in the Sunday schools. But your child will perhaps be, after ten or fifteen years, a teacher in a Sunday school. And if you will not be aware of the menace of Communism and will not fight within your church with the spiritual weapons given by Christ against the Communist menace, your sons and daughters will be before a Soviet tribunal answering for the "crime" of having taught children about Christ. Look at your children who play today and try to imagine them handcuffed, beaten, dragged before judges for having been faithful to Christ!

The defenders of Communism tell you about open churches in Moscow, in Leningrad, and the more so, in the satellite countries of Europe. They show Christian periodicals which appear in those countries as *The Journal of the Moscow Patriarchy*, *The Messenger of the Brethren*, *The Organ of the Russian Baptists*, and so on.

I am a man who believes in logic more than supposed facts, because falsities can be disguised as facts. In the Old Testament we read how Potiphar's wife showed him the clothes of Joseph, proving by this that Joseph had wished to violate her. She had the "evidence" in her hand, but the "fact" was wrong.

If anybody would show me pictures allegedly taken in hell and would make me hear tapes from hell in which Christ is praised and love is expressed and if the pictures and tapes would show the happiness of those in hell, I would not believe the pictures, I would not believe the tape, I would not believe my eyes. I would believe what logic tells me: where Satan reigns, there can be no happiness and no praise of Christ.

Communism is satanic. Even some of the closest collaborators with the Communists in the World Council of Churches told me they consider Communism to be devilish. They don't state this much publicly. They acknowledged this in discussions with me. Now, the devil would be very stupid to give freedom to the true Christian religion. Where Satan rules there can be no freedom. There exist churches, but churches which have obtained the freedom of worship only by renouncing to fulfill their duty to preach the full Gospel, which includes the denunciation of every sin and crime. They are "free" to preach that Jesus was good, but not that Karl Marx is wrong.

As the devil is an arch-liar, so the Communists are masters in lies. We have had just recently an example. In Red China, they have forbidden now Shakespeare, Beethoven, the greatest masters of human culture, and they call this "the Great Cultural Revolution." They call always evil deeds by beautiful names. They can call a new manner of Communist propaganda by the beautiful name, "Christian religion."

I come from behind the Iron Curtain. In my fatherland, Rumania, thousands of churches are open — Orthodox, Catholic, Lutheran, Baptist, and so on. When a foreigner comes he is impressed by them. He enters into an Orthodox church and the Orthodox liturgy is really very beautiful. He comes out of the church and is delighted in what he has seen. He does not know a word of the Rumanian language and does not know what is preached in these churches. I can tell him.

I will give a typical sermon as I have heard it myself in St. Catherine Church, an Orthodox church of Bucharest. The priest read the verse "Christ is our Peace." These words mean that Christ is the one who makes peace between the sinner and God. The priest explained the epistle: "Christ is our peace. Who is against peace? The American imperialists and warmongers. Who is on the side of peace? The Communist government. What do, then, the words 'Christ is our Peace' mean? They mean that Christ is on the side of the Socialist countries against Americans and so must all Christians be." This is one of the many typical sermons. A new form of Communist propaganda! Communist propaganda in religious disguise!

Religion is very powerful behind the Iron Curtain and the Communists are not so stupid as to forbid it totally. They persecute it, but at the same time they exploit it, using religion to spread their own poisonous ideology.

The average priest or pastor of the official churches in the Communist countries has to accept this compromise, sometimes after having been years in prison, either because he has been brainwashed and does not know any more to distinguish evil from good, or because he was threatened with a new imprisonment, with starvation or because his children were not allowed to study.

Other priests and pastors, if you would ask them why did they do so, would answer they have been abandoned by the West and have no other possibility.

It is not the same with the hierarchy, the religious leaders behind the Iron Curtain who serve Communism knowingly and willingly. They are used also to spread Communism in the West.

But behind the Iron Curtain there exists also another Church, a Church which has kept the full truth, and which every year gives thousands of martyrs. It is the Underground Church. Its bitter experience has taught the Underground Church to be very wise, and it has sent its members to become priests and pastors in the official church. Members of the Underground Church have attained even high ranks in the official church, and from some Communist countries, those who come as bishops to Geneva and to the National Council of Churches are secretly members of the Underground Church. The Communist secret police does not know it. They play the role as agents of the secret police, just as a Metropolitan Nikolai or the Archbishop Nikodem. They play the role of very faithful servants of Communism, but they belong to the Underground Church. And they describe to us how the western church leaders are sometimes corrupted and sometimes duped, and how, after having met them, the Communist bishops, with glasses of wine before them and prostitutes on their knees mock their western colleagues, laugh about them, and say, "We had them again; we could deceive them again." (Scenes exactly as those described by Penkovsky, of the Russian secret police, who died as a martyr for freedom, and who tells us how the political leaders of the West were duped and how the Russians rejoiced about it.)

The Communists wish to conquer America and, in order to attain this aim, they dupe American Christianity, using for this some of your shepherds.

As a man who can say about myself the words of Psalm 73:14, "All the day long have I been plagued and chastened every morning," as a man who during fourteen years has endured the Communist tortures, I fulfill my duty to the country which has received me with hospitality to be the "alarm clock" to tell you that you are in deadly danger.

As I have said already, the Underground Church from behind the Iron Curtain has its men in the Communist secret police, sometimes even in the Communist government. It has its men also in the World Council and in the National Council of Churches. It has friends everywhere who inform it. We have learned from the Bible to have our men in the very citadel of the enemy.

Only after we have been obliged to work secretly, did we understand in a new manner parts of the Bible which had been obscure for us until then. We read in St. John, 18:15, about a disciple who was known unto the high priest and who had the possibility to enter with Jesus into the much-guarded palace of the high priest. He had such an influence in this palace and was so well known by everybody there that he could speak with those who kept the door, and this was enough to bring Peter also into the court of the high priest. Those in the West will understand with difficulty such a relationship between a beloved disciple of Jesus and His murderers. We understood that we must have men in the offices of the murderers, who should appear to be friends with the murderers and inform us about their bad intentions.

I have made a test. I wrote a letter to one of the top leaders of the World Council of Churches in America which contained some information about the secret Orthodox Underground movement in Rumania. He immediately answered that he had sent this letter to Geneva. Now, one of the secretaries of the Lutheran World Foundation told me that he had to destroy a cable which I had sent to Geneva because the mail there is not secure. There are the Soviet spies who read every letter which arrives there. To send a letter to Geneva means to give it in the hands of the Soviet spies. We should not forget that a man of the Russian secret police, the priest Borovoi, is on the permanent staff of the World Council of Churches and he, the representative of the murderers of Christians, is Vice-Chairman of the Committee for Religious Liberty! To Geneva, where the Soviet spies do just what they like, has been sent a letter with secret information about an Underground movement in the Communist camp!

Happily I foresaw this, and all the information and all the names which I gave had the characteristics which were necessary to mislead the secret police and its accomplices. I wished to test only once again the unreliability of every Christian leader who is in any way connected with the World Council of Churches, and I had the proof that it is so.

Never believe the Communists or their accomplices!

I come from behind the Iron Curtain. We have seen in Rumania how they know to lie. The first day when the Soviet troops entered in our country, they put posters on the streets. In these posters they assured the Rumanian population that they have no intention to change the social order in Rumania and that, after defeating Nazism, the Soviet troops will withdraw to their own country. But after a very short time, Vishinsky, Deputy Foreign Secretary, entered into the office of our king, beat his fist on his table and ordered him to nominate a Communist government. Nobody in our country was on the side of the Communists, but the Russians imposed upon us a Communist government, disarming first our army and our police. Our king resisted with dignity as much as he could, but abandoned by America and Great Britain, he had to yield in the end. Nobody has chosen the Communists. Never has any nation chosen in free elections the Communists to be their rulers.

Now they were at power, but they had nobody behind them and, in order to be able to rule, they began to deceive. They made demonstrations on the street with the slogan, "Long Live the King," because they knew the King to be popular with us. A very short time afterwards, when they had all the institutions in their hands, they drove the King out of the country.

Knowing our people to be very religious, the Communists played the role of being religious themselves. Just as Italian and American Communists say now they can be friends with the Catholics and with the Protestants and everybody, so the Communists said at that time: "Oh, the Russian Communists have done it badly. They have persecuted religion, but we will not be like this." I saw myself Teohari Georgeseu, the Communist Minister of Interior Affairs, making the sign of the Cross in the Orthodox church and kissing the holy images. They convened in our parliament building a Congress with 4,000 bishops, priests, pastors, preachers, rabbis, of all religions and there the Communist Prime Minister Groza delivered a speech assuring the clergymen that they, the new Communist government, will be entirely on the side of religion, that they will pay good salaries to the priests and pensions to the retired ones, that they will encourage religion. Four thousand priests and pastors cheered this Communist minister, believing in what he said. There was only one pastor who stood up and openly protested saying that the role of a Christian clergyman is to glorify Christ, not transitory rulers. This lone pastor told everyone that we must not believe the wolves disguised in sheepskins. This one pastor was sentenced afterwards to twenty-five years of prison. The speech in the parliament was one of the charges against him. But he had a consolation. He was not alone in prison. The bishops and priests who had cheered the Communists and who decided to collaborate with them, came to prison, too. They were sentenced just like him, tortured just like him. But there was one difference: the pastor who had protested had a peaceful conscience. He was serene. He knew he had fulfilled his duty, whereas the other pastors and priests condemned themselves for having been deceived. God has given me the grace to be that lone pastor.

Behind the Iron Curtain there exists one force which has opposed Communism from its very beginning. It is the Underground Church of Russia, of China, and of the European satellite countries. This Underground Church is the only hope of one-third of the world. And as the whole world is threatened by Communism, this Underground Church is the great hope for the whole world. It is the national interest of America, it is the interest of Western civilization, it is the interest of the universal church, to do its utmost to support this Underground Church in the Communist camp. It is the only organized opposition to Communist lands.

But some Western church leaders, and especially American ones, do their utmost to muzzle the voice of this Underground Church. Denunciators and traitors, who are leaders of the official churches in Communist lands are received with great honor in your country. As I told one of the top men of the World Council of Churches, who, after recognizing himself that, "Wurmbrand is a man who has been imprisoned for the Gospel's sake fourteen years," wrote to all his churches that I should not be allowed to preach. The real motive of this is that he is afraid for his churches to hear the message of the Underground Church from behind the Iron Curtain. Never has any member of the Underground Church, who has escaped to the West, been received in Geneva. Never have they been invited to say what they have to say. There are church leaders who do their utmost to hide the tortures inflicted by Communists on Christians.

The loss to the Western Church by not hearing the voice of the Underground Church in the Communist camp is huge. Because of this indifference they are kept misinformed about the Communist menace to themselves.

But there is something else. Just as oysters produce pearls when some foreign object enters the shell (pearls being nothing else than the tears of the oyster), so the Underground Church, because of its much suffering in fifty years of jails and tortures, has produced pearls of exquisite Christian souls. They have a depth of knowledge of God which is unknown to your modern theologians who every year invent some "new" theology. These precious pearls of the Kingdom remain unknown to the Western Church.

In suffering, the leaders and the martyrs of the Underground Church have received unusual gifts and powers of the Holy Spirit. For example, we were in prison cells, gravely sick. I myself have been sick in prison of backbone, lung, and intestinal tuberculosis. We had no medicine. We had no food. We had little air. We were beaten, but God has healed me. Doctors who examined me in Oslo said that according to their medical books, I should be dead, because four vertebrae and the whole surface of both lungs has been attacked by tuberculosis. They wondered how I am alive. I am alive by the miraculous gifts of the Holy Spirit which God has imparted to the Underground Church as a reward for its faithfulness in suffering. Innumerable others have been healed in the same way. All these gifts remain lost for the Church as long as some of your church leaders put a wall of partition between your church and the Underground Church and muzzle the voice of the Underground Church.

You should not allow this crime to be perpetrated! Ask from your church leaders fellowship with the Underground Church behind the Iron Curtain! Ask your church leaders to put you in touch with the most valuable representatives whom Christ has today in the world!

The Underground Church consists of men who have seen with their own eyes the signs and the wonders and the mighty hand and the stretched out arm of the Lord. She has a message which can save your Christian faith, which can save your church, your freedom, your country and your civilization.

Americans, your future is at stake.

I have just had my first Thanksgiving day in America. I was in church, then I was in a Christian home. I received guests in my home. Everybody in America was so happy on that day. My wife and I wept.

As we are refugees, some friends brought us a few sheets and blankets, towels and handkerchiefs. When my wife saw these things, she began to weep. She had been a prisoner, too. During bitter winters she had to shovel the earth, and she remembers that she had never had a handkerchief. Those who have not passed through this cannot imagine the bitterness of shoveling the earth in winter and not having a handkerchief. We remember what it meant to us in winter to have the hands handcuffed behind our backs, and not to be able to wipe our nose. For you, Thanksgiving day was a day of joy. We could not rejoice like the others, not only because we remember the things through which we have passed, but knowing that thousands of our brethren and sisters in faith are passing through the same and much worse things just now.

A friendly family brought us a turkey and put it in the refrigerator. The man turned smilingly towards us and said: "Now you have also a turkey in the refrigerator." I shuddered. I began to weep when I remembered that I have been in the "refrigerator cell" as prisoner. In the prison of Gherla in Rumania, there existed a refrigerating cell in which we were kept for hours until the heart nearly stopped beating. Then we were taken out, we were warmed again. And then, finally warmed, were put in the refrigerator again.

I could not rejoice as you rejoice remembering not only what has happened to me, but what is happening to thousands of Christians today.

Americans, this is the future which the Communists and their accomplices prepare for your children.

In Russia there is a law which permits the Communists to take the children away from their Christian parents in order to avoid the poisoning of these children, as they say, with the false Christian doctrine. Children have been taken away from innumerable Christians in Russia and given to Communist orphanages where they are taught to hate the notion of God and of Christ. Their parents are not allowed even to see them.

Americans, your fate will be tragic if you will not counteract Communism in your country. Don't be lulled to the deadly menace by certain of your church leaders who work day and night to soften your opposition to Communism, to cause you to forget its dangers!

Is it not true that every church leader who praises Communism — which now kills American youth in Vietnam — betrays America? Between Communism and Christianity there is a life and death struggle. Anyone who would have praised Nazism during war time would have betrayed a vital interest of America. Is the same thing not true of those church leaders who praise Communism while it is killing your youth?

The Church can never have peaceful co-existence with Communism any more than it can have peaceful co-existence with prostitution, drug addiction or murder; any more than the FBI can co-exist with gangsterism.

Is it not true that every church leader who asks for the admission of the bandit Mao-Tse-Tung and his blood-drenched representatives in the UN, while not saying one word of protest against the torturing and murdering of Christians in Red China, betrays the Church and America?

I know that I am a very insignificant Christian, but you hear through me the warning of those who cannot speak for themselves — the warning of the Underground Church which speaks out of fifty years of Communist torture and killings. It is this Underground Church which is the only effective opposition in Communist lands today. It is this Church which warns you that if you do not help it, its fate may well be yours.

Consciously or unconsciously, some American church leaders work day and night at the softening of America's resistance to Communism, at the lulling to sleep of its people.

To me, this is betrayal.

It is betrayal of the millions of Americans who will pay the price we have paid in Rumania.

It is betrayal of their children who will suffer what our children have suffered.

It is betrayal of the enslaved of the world who look to America as hope for the future.

Apostate Churchianity may enter into an agreement with Communism, but Christianity will never do so.

Americans, learn from our tragedy!

Americans, remember Pearl Harbor!

DRAWINGS OF PRISON LIFE

"Our heavy chains were struck off in the stone-flagged courtyard, and we were goaded with blows along dark passages thick with dirt. My companions were thrust, in small groups, into cells along a gallery. Loud protests came from inside them: 'There's no room here! We're suffocating already!'

A hard push in the spine sent me stumbling forward and the door clanged behind me. The stench in the cell made me feel sick. At first I could see nothing. I felt about, and my hands drew back from a ghastly, naked, sweating body. Slowly, as I grew used to the dim light from a ceiling bulb, I saw four rows of bunks rising in their tiers on each side of the cell, with men who lay gasping for breath. More men, also half-naked, sat on the floor, or leaned against the walls. No-one could move without waking a neighbor. In all there were one hundred of us.

My stay in this cell over the next months was broken only by journeys to the stinking sump outside, carrying lavatory pails."

"In the weeks that followed, I went through the whole Secret Police gamut. I was given the water torture, in which water is poured down a funnel until the stomach is bursting; then it is kicked. I was left for hours with two wolf-dogs who leapt at the slightest movement. They were trained not to bite, but their yelping and snarling and the snap of the fangs an inch from the throat kept you rigid with fright."

"For fourteen years of prison, our food was horribly bad. Prisoners were forced to eat their own excrements and to drink urine. For much of the time, we ate cabbage and unwashed intestines."

"In our cells, Christians were tied to crosses. Every day the crosses were put on the floor. Then dozens of other prisoners were obligated to fulfill their bodily necessities upon the faces and upon the bodies of the crucified ones. Then the crosses were erected for the amusement of the Communists who stood around jeering: 'Look at your Christ; how beautiful He is!' "

"When they could not force us to betray our brethren by all their interrogations and tortures, they would beat our children before our very eyes — and even to death if that were necessary."

"Tape recorders, with what we were certain were the
screams of our wives being beaten, were played in
the cell corridors, often driving us to distraction.
Other days, cats were hung by their back legs just
outside our tiny cell windows. In time they began
to scream and cry pitifully, while we covered our
ears and buried our heads in our arms.
They left them to wail until they died."

"I worked out a routine to which I kept for the next two years. I stayed awake all night. When the 10 p.m. bell signalled time to sleep, I began my program. Sometimes I was sad, sometimes cheerful, but the nights were not long enough — there was so much to do."

"I began with a prayer in which tears, often of thankfulness, were seldom absent."

"Next, I preached a sermon as I would in church, but with complete truth, no longer caring what anyone, save God, thought."

"Every night I talked to my wife and son."

"Each night I passed an hour living in the minds of my chief adversaries."

"The Communists believe that happiness comes from material satisfaction; but in our cells, cold, hungry and in rags, we danced for joy . . . and to retain our sanity . . . every night."

" 'We do the beatings,' said Brinzaru with a show of yellow
teeth. 'But your American friends give us the tools.'
He displayed his own favorite, a long, black rubber truncheon.
'Read the label.' It was inscribed MADE IN U.S.A.,
then he sent me back to my cell to think about it."

"In our country, Christians have been stripped naked and have been obligated to crawl on the floor with their hands handcuffed on the back, and on the floor were hundreds of pieces of splintered glass. Whipped, they had to crawl on this splintered glass until their bodies were torn into ribbons."

"My solitary cell was deep underground. A light bulb shone from the ceiling on bare walls, an iron bedstead with three planks and a straw pallet. Stale air entered through a pipe high in the wall. There was no bucket and I had to wait always for the guard to take me to the latrine. This was the worst imposition for every prisoner who suffered it. Sometimes they made you wait for hours, laughing at your pleadings. Men, and women too, went without food and water for fear of increasing their agony. I myself have eaten from the dish in which I fulfilled my needs, without washing it, because I had no water. I was kept in solitary confinement in this cell for the next two years."

''My cell was twelve paces round: I shuffled around it in torn socks. 'Faster!' shouted the guard. 'Keep moving!' When at last I fell sprawling, the guard charged in and cracked me across the elbow with a club as I struggled up. The pain was so agonizing that I fell again. 'Get up! Get moving! This isn't a rest cure. This is the menage!' ''

"In suffering, the leaders and the martyrs of the Underground
Church have received unusual gifts and powers of the Holy
Spirit. For example, we were in prison cells, gravely sick. I
myself have been sick in prison of backbone, lung, and
intestinal tuberculosis. We had no medicine, we had no food.
We had little air. We were beaten, but God has healed me.
For thirty months I lay in Room 4, the room from
which, it was said, no man ever emerged alive!"

"I have seen fellow-prisoners in Communist prisons
beaten, with fifty pounds of chains on their legs —
praying for America . . . that the dike will not
crumple; that it will remain free."

LETTERS TO CHURCH LEADERS

Letter to a Catholic Archbishop

To His Eminence

The Archbishop of................................

Eminence,

I was surely very pleased to have had the opportunity of speaking with a prominent personality of the Catholic Church in America.

But in a short conversation not all things could be said. I consider it as my duty to write to you the following.

With us, in Rumania, a canal has been built by slave labour. 200,000 men and women worked at it, hungry, beaten. Thousands died. At the canal men ate rats and snakes. My own wife has eaten there grass as the cattle.

At this canal, there was the so-called "religious unit", an unit of extermination. In it were bishops, priests, pastors of all denominations, or, as we call them of all "damnations" (Christ has meant us to be one). But there were not only clergymen. Farmers, young boys, everyone who was in prison for his faithfulness to Christ was put in this unit, which had as overseers common criminals, to whom release has been promised if they will torture the Christians.

This promise has never been kept, but the criminals, having the vain hope of freedom, competed in torturing Christians. Woe to the one caught crossing himself, folding his hands for prayer or saying a word about Christ! He had to pay with blood for this.

One Sunday morning, the political officer of the canal, came to inspect the unit and called out, just at random, a young man. He asked him: "What have you been?" He answered: "I have been and am still a Catholic priest." The Communist asked him then in mockery: "Do you still believe in Christ?" The priest was silent a few seconds, seconds long as eternity, because eternity was decided in those seconds. Then his face began to shine. I believe in the Transfiguration. I have seen it. And the priest opened his mouth. He did not speak yet. But in that moment I understood a Bible verse, which had seemed always very queer to me. St. Matthew writes in the preamble to the Sermon on the Mount "Jesus opened His mouth and spoke." What sense have these words? Nobody can speak with a shut mouth. Now I understood. On the Mount then, the same thing had happened, which I saw before my eyes.

The opening of the mouth had been a gesture apart. The priest had only opened his mouth. He did not speak yet, but an awe overcame us all. We knew that then a pearl would come out of his mouth.

Then the priest said with a very humble, but very decided voice: "Mr. Lieutenant, when I became a priest, I knew that during church history thousands of priests have been killed for their faith. Notwithstanding I became a priest. I knew what I become. And as often as I ascended to the altar, dressed in the beautiful priestly robe, I promised to God that, if I will wear the uniform of a prisoner, I will serve Him, too. Mr. Lieutenant, prison is a very poor argument against religion. I love Christ from all my heart."

I am sorry that I cannot convey the intonation wherewith he said the words "I love Christ". It was like hearing Juliet speaking about Romeo. We, the others, were ashamed, because we believed in Christ. This man loved Him as a bride loves her bridegroom.

The lieutenant asked him further: "And do you believe still in the Pope, too?" The priest, knowing very well that his answers may cost his life, replied what was his belief: "Since St. Peter there has always been a Pope. And until Jesus will come back, there will always be a Pope. The actual Pope (it was Pius the XIIth) has not shaken hands with you and never will a Pope do it."

This man has afterwards been horribly tortured. Then he disappeared. It is unprobable that he is still alive. He has given his young life not only for his faith in Christ, but also for his faith in the Pope.

What a shock must it be for him wherever he is, in this or in another life, to find out that he has been mistaken. The Pope has shaken hands first with Gromiko, then with Podgornii, members of the Soviet Government, which has jailed and killed thousands of Catholics and millions of other Christians. He has shaken hands with the ones who have closed innumerable churches and poison Catholic youth with atheism.

The crimes cannot be put on Stalin alone. When Stalin killed Christians, Podgornii, Gromiko, Breshnev and the others have been his executioners. The Pope has accepted the blood-stained hand of the murderers, instead of publicly denouncing them and taking the side of martyrs.

In Red China, in the district of Ten Sheen, four Catholic priests have been buried alive. In Canton, Catholic nuns have been put to trample on crosses. All the churches have been closed and desecrated with pictures of Mao-Tse-Tung. While these things happened, the Catholic Bishops of America came together and decided the weighty matter that it is allowed to eat meat on

Friday. They did not say one word of solidarity with the victims of Communism. They did not protest. I saw in the pictures the smiling faces of these bishops, I saw your own smiling face and I wondered: "Do you belong to the same church, to the same body with the martyrs? How is it then that your face does not express their suffering? Is it not so in a body that, if one member suffers, all the other members with it?"

I have attended innumerable religious services in Catholic churches of America. I have heard mentioned the saints of centuries ago, whom I respect highly, too, but very rarely did anybody mention in his sermon the saints and heroes of today's Catholic Church, who die for their faith in the Communist camp.

I read Pope Paul's speech before what is falsely called the Organization of United Nations. In fact it is an organization of some disunited nations. And, then, the nations of 1/3 of the world are not represented in it. Those seated there are not the representatives of the Russian, Rumanian, Bulgarian or Polish nation, but the oppressors of these nations, the mass-killers of Christians. I myself don't believe at all in the Organization of United Nations. A school cannot be lead according to the principles of democracy. Only the teachers have to decide, not the pupils by majority of votes. In a hospital, not the vote of patients decides, but the doctor alone. The United States, Great Britain, and the Congo (in which missionaries have been eaten only two years ago), Gabon, Laos and Sierra Leone should not decide by a majority of votes. This would allow that the illiterate and undeveloped nations, because they are many, will decide the future of the world. There exist teacher — and pupil — nations. The most civilized have to decide. The United States become powerless to be useful if they need always the consent of analphabetes and cannibals.

But anyhow, the Pope, supposed by you to be the vicar of Christ, spoke before the assembly. He spoke words of respect and appraisal for all the representatives there, not making any distinction between Christians, rulers who give freedom to Christianity and those who kill Christians. He put them all in one pot, gave the same respect to all, expressed his conviction that lovers of freedom and gangsters who have stolen whole countries by deceit and terror seek peace and gave to all of them the same benediction. Did Jesus not make any difference between Herod, the Pharisees, innocent children and His disciples? Is this not misleading? Should the Pope not have expressed his solidarity with today's martyrs? Should the Pope not have protested against the killing of his own flock? Should he not have used the pulpit of the Organization of United Nations to alert peoples about the menace of Communism for the West? That is what the suffering Catholics behind the Iron and Bamboo Curtain had the right to expect from him. He has failed.

Misleading has been also the encyclic of the defunct Pope John XXIII, "Peace on earth". Seduction and love use the same language. If I love a girl and wish her as my wife, I tell her "I love you". If I wish a girl only for one night, to throw her away afterwards as a dirty rag, I tell her the same words, "I love you". The same with the word, "Peace". Every gangster wonders why the Police do not give him peace. He has stolen and wonders why the Police are after him. A gangster steals a purse. The Communists have stolen countries with one billion inhabitants. Never has any nation chosen the Communists as rulers, in free elections. They are gangsters on an international scale. They are all for peace. They should remain with what they have stolen and they should prepare in peace their next step forward. That is what they understand by "peace". For Christians the notion of "peace" is connected with that of "justice". Peace is established when the gangster receives his deserved punishment and what has been stolen is restored to the legitimate owner.

Pope John pleaded for "peace", not taking a clear stand against Communism, for the enslaved peoples. By this he, too, mislead Christians.

The very title of the Pope is "Pontifex maximus". Pontifex means in Latin "maker of bridges". Every Christian is a maker of bridges. By tears, supplications and self-sacrifices, every Christian constructs bridges on which the sinner may pass from abysses to heaven. Sinners and criminals have all the love and aid of Christians, to be saved. But only sinners and criminals have it, never the sin and the crime. Communists must be loved, but not their sin: Communism. Jesus taught us to hate the sin and to love the sinner. With the last Popes, as with some leaders of the Protestant world, we have complacency towards Communism, instead of love towards the men united with hatred against their godless system.

There exists no possibility to build a bridge which should unite crime with righteousness.

The Pope concludes now concordates with Communist countries, when the Vatican before this has excommunicated bishops for the slightest step of cooperation with the Communists. Is this right?

As is to be expected, I don't believe the Pope to be the Vicar of Christ. But the Pope should believe in papal infallibility. The Pope should respect what a Pope saith. Therefore I will quote to you the sayings of Popes about Communism:

PIUS THE IX in "QUI PLURIBUS" (1846):

"Communism is a b s o l u t e l y contrary to the natural law itself and, if once adopted, would utterly destroy the rights, property and possessions of all men and even society itself". (Concordats with those who destroy all rights.)

POPE LEON XIII IN "QUOD APOSTOLICE MUNERIS" (1878).

"Communism is the fatal plague which insinuates itself into the very marrow of human society only to bring about its ruin." (Concordats with a plague which ruins. Why should doctors not arrive to peaceful agreements with other plagues like cholera?)

POPE PIUS XI IN "ATHEISTIC COMMUNISM" (1937)

"Communism strips man of his liberty, robs human personality of all its dignity and removes all the moral restraints that check the eruptions of blind impulse."

These are just sayings of Popes and as they are not "ex cathedra", they may not be considered as infallible by Catholics.

But now I will remind you of a decree, the Decree of the Supreme Congregation of the Holy Office of the Catholic Church, dated the 2nd of July 1949:

"The faithful who profess the materialist and anti-Christian doctrine of the Communists and especially those who defend and propagate them, incur ipso facto, as apostates from the Catholic faith, excommunication specially reserved to the Holy See."

This decree is binding not only for those who are submitted to the Holy See, but also for the one who sits on it.

There arises only one problem. Is it a crime to practice with the wolf only when he appears as a wolf? Or is it the more so a crime to practice with him, when the wolf appears disguised in a sheepskin? Should not a church leader be able to distinguish between a real sheep and a wolf in disguise?

Communists appear now in disguise, as propagandists of universal peace, provided that they remain with what they have stolen and are free to prepare the future leap forwards of the world revolution. Communists, they who have uprooted the Tibetan people, they who practice anti-semitism, who have deported hundreds of thousands to Siberia for the crime of being Lithuanians, Hebrews, Germans and Rumanians, who persecute men because of religion, they, who have reduced peoples to a level of starvation pretend to fight against poverty. Must they not be demasked? Must the sheep not be alerted about this new device?

Catholics and Protestants have now the fashion of dialogues with the Marxists. Why do the Marxists have dialogues only with the Christians in the West? Why do they forbid the proclamation of the whole Christian truth in their countries? Why don't they have dialogues with cardinals Wyszinsky and Mindzenthy? Why don't they go to the other world to have dialogues with the millions of Christians killed by them? Christians can have dialogues with nobody. A professor of mathematics does not discuss with his disciples the truths of mathematics. He announces them and they have to accept. So Christians have a definitive truth revealed by God. They proclaim it; it is not a matter of discussion.

By every attitude of complacency towards Communism, by your silence about the Communist terror, by discussing meat on Friday while the blood of your brethren is shed, as the Pharisees gave tithes of little things and left undone the weighty matters of the law, you trod on blood of martyrs.

When I told you a few of these things, you bowed your head and said: "We are inexcusable". I hope that you will not remain at this feeling of shame, but that this will be transformed in action.

You cannot build in the same time bridges towards the sheep and towards the wolves. You must be whole-heartedly on the side of the oppressed or on the side of the oppressor. You cannot have it both ways. Clear stand must be taken.

Behind the Iron Curtain there exists a very earnest ecumenism. Calvin taught us that in Catholicism not everything is wrong. You believe in the Holy Trinity, you have the Bible as a holy book, you recite the same creed as we. There are only some of your dogmas wherewith we, the Protestants, do not agree. But usually, the Catholic Christians behind the Iron Curtain suffer persecution for the essentials of the faith which they have in common with us, not for what divides us. In the essentials, Christians in Communist lands unite in fight and suffering. This is an ecumenism to which I subscribe.

But an ecumenism between Catholic churchleaders who do not care for the martyr church in one-third of the world and Protestant leaders who are of the same type is ungodly.

In the early church, Rome had a place of honor because it gave the greatest number of martyrs. This is true today about the Underground Church in the Communist countries. The voice of the Underground Church should be listened to, and Christians of all confessions should join hands with her in her heroical fight for Christ against Communism.

With Christian love,
R. Wurmbrand

Excerpts from a
Letter to a Leader of the World Council of Churches
Dear Brother:

My name may be unknown to you. I am a Lutheran Pastor of Rumanian origin who has worked in the representation of the World Council of Churches in Rumania. Afterwards I was in Rumanian prisons for 14 years, one of the main charges against me being that I represented what was considered at that time the imperialist spy organization, The World Council of Churches.

I was ransomed from Rumania by the Norwegian Israel mission and the Hebrew Christian Alliance. Now I am, for a short time, in the United States, where I have tried thus far unsuccessfully, to get an appointment with you until June.

I avoided writing to the World Council of Churches in Geneva for a long time, not wishing to put it under a material obligation towards me, but after I managed to secure my daily bread, I did it, out of a heart full of sorrow.

This sorrow came when I read an article in the International Review of Missions, published by the World Council of Churches in the January, 1966 issue in which it is written, that "the Orthodox Church and Protestantism are growing in Rumania in an atmosphere of complete religious liberty." I asked Mr. Visser't Hooft that if this assertion is true, then I would like to have answers to the following questions:

1.   What is the address of the Bible Society in Rumania? (no Bible Society permitted in Rumania.) Could he show me one Bible published during the past 20 years in Rumania?

2.   Could he name one book published by a Protestant during the last 20 years?

3.   What is the address of the YMCA in Rumania?

4.   Could he give me the address and the hour of one Sunday school for children conducted in Bucharest?

5.   What is the name and address of one charitable Christian organization in Rumania?

6.   Where can I hear one Christian broadcast in Rumania?

7.   Where are the pastors, Vacareanu, Nailescu, Ghelbegeanu and others? (They are in prison for their faith.)

There are many other similar questions which I would like to ask him.

Why are deliberate lies told which mock the suffering of my fatherland and the suffering of its church?

If my barber had been put in prison for theft and would have come out, I would have gone to see him and would have helped him and asked him about his experiences in prison. I, a Rumanian pastor, after 14 years in prison, when one of the main charges against me was that I worked for the World Council of Churches, and I was asked nothing about my experiences and what I know about the situation in Rumania.

The Archbishop Moisescu, about whom even the sparrows in Rumania know that he is a traitor and a man of the secret police, was banqueted in Geneva. I was in prison with 400 Christians — denounced by this same Moisescu. He reports about what happens in Rumania. To me brother Visser t'Hooft sends very kind greetings, but has never asked to speak to me.

Bishop Hromadka, an arch-traitor who went to Moscow and was praised by Mikoyan, the right-hand man of Stalin in the mass murders of Christians, is another one who was banqueted at Geneva. But I was never given a hearing. Nobody asked me how am I living, whether I have enough to eat. (I do not need this) as I am supplied with food, but it would have been very normal to ask me this, too). But what is more important, they did not ask me about what is happening in Rumania and how the Christians there are faring.

The hearts of the Rumanian Christians are bleeding, knowing that their traitors and denunciators are embraced in Geneva and yet they are not given a chance to tell what is happening. Very politely I was told, "Please don't come to Geneva, because the Communists will know and be irked," just as if the Communists are dictating in Geneva too and not only in the Soviet camp.

I asked English Church Leaders, "Why have you eaten at banquets with our inquisitors?" The answer was: "We are Christians and must have friendship and fellowship with everybody, including the Communists." And I was asked if I do not agree with this Christian attitude.

I am a man who has not read the Bible for 14 years. For 14 years I have never had a book or a piece of paper in my hands. So, surely others must know the Bible better than I do. However I faintly remember that it is written in the Bible, "friendship with the world is hatred towards God." But even putting aside what the Bible says, I asked again, "Supposing that we must have friendship and fellowship with everybody, why do you have friendship only with our inquisitors and none with their victims?"

A high British clergyman and all the others who were with him and like him, wined and dined with our inquisitors and our betrayers. He did not leave even $100.00 for the families of Christian martyrs. The World Council of Churches and the other great bodies represented by them have never had fellowship with these. These have never experienced the love of these Christian organizations. But the Communists have. Does not the love of God extend to the bad and to the good? The love of these men however, went only to the torturers of Christians.

I do not speak in my name (I am only a very insignificant man, and have been with the weak and little ones in prison), but I was there with heroes and saints to whom I did not dare to lift my eyes, whose shoelaces I was not worthy to tie. There were pastors in prison about whom one had the feeling that merely to touch their garment was to be made whole. Yet their children were starving at home; many of them died.

They did not see anything of the fellowship and the friendship which the World Council of Churches and the great Christian bodies are showing to their inquisitors.

I speak for those who cannot speak for themselves, because they continue to be kept in chains. I am an unworthy man, but I speak for the worthiest of the Christians of the 20th century. We have had in Rumania saints and heroes like these of the first Christian centuries. Instead of their names being published everywhere in the publications of the World Council of Churches, I have always found only the names of the traitors and to them were extended words of "understanding" and "friendship" — to these, the murderers of Christians.

I wonder why the Archbishop of Canterbury went to see the Pope, who is healthy and does not need his visit. He was in Rome, but why did he not go to see the graves of Catholic bishops who died in prison in Rumania? Why did he not put a flower on their graves and shed a tear there? Why did he not speak privately with one of the Protestant bishops of Rumania?

I speak from the bleeding heart of Rumanian Christians who have been, are, and continuing to be persecuted. We see our children poisoned by atheism, our youth being brainwashed. It may seem mad to you, but priests have been forced in our prisons to say the holy mass over excrements and urine and Christians have been forced to take communion in this way. Priests and ministers have been forced to commit the most obscene and degenerate acts which I cannot put down in writing.

If you have the slightest doubt that such horrible tortures are being inflicted, come and see my body — it speaks more than all the words which I can say. It is not only the tortured body of a man, but you will see in me the body of the Rumanian people and the Rumanian Church which has been tortured and still is.

I have tried to speak with the leaders at the National Council of Churches. I have tried to speak with you. I have been unsuccessful. I was told, and I believe it, that your schedule is full and that you have only just time for lunch and dinner. I did not eat lunch or dinner for 14 years, and I think that Church leaders should impose upon themselves days of fasting, and be prepared to listen to those who have suffered and to see that their duty is to fight Communism which tortures Christians and not to make friendship and have fellowship with them.

I know that an insignificant pastor such as I am does not as a rule write such a letter to high church leaders. All this may sound abnormal to you, but I speak out of an abnormal situation, from a situation of a church which has arrived at the paroxysm of suffering.

Hromadka shook hands with Mikoyan. Did he know that 150 Baptist pastors were recently deported to Siberia by Mikoyan? We have the list of these 150 pastors.

I have poured out before you the suffering of my Church. I will never be healthy again, because instead of trying to forget what I have passed through, I must re-open my wounds every time when I tell others about the suffering of our Church, your Church and mine.

In the past much has been said about peaceful co-existence. I am not a politician and I do not know what is the best policy, but I know that if states can have peaceful co-existence with the international gangsters of Communism, church bodies can never peacefully co-exist with atheism and they must fight it to the utmost.

Please excuse the style of this letter. It was written by a man who during the 14 years of imprisonment may have lost his manners. A suffering soul has cried to you. Jesus has always received such cries with compassion. Please receive it in the same manner and see if you can arrange for us to meet as early as possible. I enclose a schedule of my appointments, also a Certificate which will explain to you in detail who I am. I anticipate your reply.

Mr. Visser't Hooft never answered my letter. I wonder if he would have left unanswered a letter from the traitor Justin Moisescu.

Try to put yourself in my place and think how I felt when I came to the National Council of Churches and while I waited in the lobby I looked through the periodicals edited by the National Council. For a man who had read nothing in 14 years, the first thing that met my eye was an article in which the National Council defends Prof. Althizer against the Methodist bishop who wished to exclude him from the university. The periodical of the National Council said that it is the right of a professor of theology to say that "God is Dead". If God had been dead we all would have been dead long ago. We lived 14 years by God's hand. Christian prisoners were tied on crosses. The crosses were put on the floor and three times a day other prisoners were compelled to relieve themselves upon the faces and bodies of these men and then the cross was erected again.

If these Christians had not had the living God near them at that time, they would not have survived and their faith would not have survived.

The second thing I read was that the National Council asks America to admit Red China into the organization of the U. N., but there was not one word about the suffering of the Chinese Christians.

At the last session of the World Council of Churches in March, a decision was taken which seems very strange to me. "The World Council of Churches invites America to stop its fight with Communism and also invites the Eastern States to stop its striving to overthrow by force the regimes all over the world." There was however one difference. In Eastern Europe, nobody published your resolutions. Nobody knows about them in the East. So while you disarm morally only the West, the East knows nothing about you. It is like disarming a policeman while he fights against gangsters in the hope that the gangsters will give up robbery, but the gangsters don't even listen to you.

I possess a letter of the Central Committee of the Chinese Communist Party to the Communist Party of China in which it shows how Communists should win the leadership of churches.[1] Are the Communists now striving consciously to have the World Council of Churches in their hands and did they not succeed to a great extent?

I hope to hear from you at your earliest convenience and look forward to speaking to you personally. In the meantime I remain

Respectfully and devotedly your brother in Christ,

Richard Wurmbrand

1)   This is published on page 163

Excerpts of a second letter to this same leader of the W.C.C.

I, before speaking with a man, make of him the object of quiet meditation, until meditation is transformed in contemplation, until I see his soul divested of body and detached of transitory circumstances, as it will stay once before the Judge. I see him not as he is now, but as he will be then, regretting every sin, as I regretted them in deep repentance in years of solitary confinement. This makes me love him. I wish you happy in the eternal paradise, which surely exists. I would not be happy if you would not be happy there, too. I meditate daily before the crucifix and I know how much Jesus craves that you may be not only saved, but exalted, how He thirsts for your soul.

With these sentiments I spoke to you on the 9th. With these sentiments I write.

"I was in prison and you have not come to see me." This reproach I can make to all Western religious leaders who have visited the Communist countries in the last years. You have not even asked to see the thousands of Christian prisoners; you have not come to see their families, which hungered. The more, some of us came out in the West. Here the World Council of Churches never asked us what we eat, neither have you asked me. I don't possess in this whole world a bed, a sheet, a blanket, a spoon of my own. And as me are many others. I saw you after so many years of unspeakable suffering. Neither you, nor other religious leaders (with rare exceptions) had one word of consolation for me or a word which would strengthen my faith so weakened in the many tribulations. We are His little ones. You have neglected your duty towards us all.

Pastor Milan Haimovici of Rumania has been in prison 7 years for having worked in behalf of the World Council of Churches. He has suffered great tortures to give accusatory statements against others and he did not give. He came out of Rumania. Nobody of the World Council of Churches cared for him. A Bulgarian pastor, Popov, is now in Sweden after 13 years in Communist prisons. The World Council of Churches had not a good word or a cent for him.

At the last Presbyterian convention, as in all the sittings of the World Council of Churches, it was decided to build bridges towards the Communist world. Towards the 1 billion people oppressed by the Communists, leaders of American Churches build no bridges. We did not feel your concern.

Our conversation has been dramatic. I told you harsh words, but we embraced also each other and prayed together. It was because I love you, whereas others hate and attack you. Nathan charged David of grave crimes, but did it out of love.

How should I qualify the decision of the last Presbyterian convention to build bridges towards Communism "with the risk of endangering the national security of America"? What has the couple Rosenberg done? They also built a bridge towards Communism, endangering the national security of America. They were electrocuted. And now the Presbyterian convention tries to build the same bridge. The National and World Council of Churches and many other denominations do the same!

What makes me weep is that the next day after the publishing of such shameful decisions, there were no demonstrations of millions of Americans with high patriotic feeling to protest against them and that the church leaders remained in their places.

Jesus teaches us to love our enemies. The murderer of my family has been converted in my house. I have brought to Christ some of my Communist jailors. I know what love towards enemies means. But how will I love an enemy if I don't love from all my heart my own country and nation? To endanger the national security of America is not a phrase. It means to endanger the lives of millions of men.

1 billion men live under terrible oppression. The Communists have published that they have killed millions of innocent Christians, putting the charge on Stalin. But where were Mikoyan, Breshnev, Gromyko, etc. at that time? They were Stalin's executioners. On the other side there is the world of freedom for the Christians and its main support — America. I have seen innumerable Christians dying in prison not only with hope in Christ, but also with hope in America that it will free once our country. The national security of America is a wealth of the whole free world. You endanger this in order to build bridges towards the mass murderers of Christians? Towards those who poison with atheism hundreds of millions of children? Who makes to stumble one of

the little ones would better be thrown in the depth of the sea. What about those who do it with millions of little ones? How have you no holy wrath against these killers of bodies and souls?

You tried to repair things: "the national security of America, too". No, only of America! Because in the East nobody publishes the resolutions of the World Council of Churches and those of the Presbyterian convention and other Western religious leaders, and nobody cares for them. You disarm only the world of liberty, although you say that you are on its side and that you are an anti-Communist. Why don't you say this openly and often?

You said that I do wrong to publish all the tortures to which Communists submit Christians, because this will make people hate the Communists. Whosoever has heard my preaching knows, that I propagate hatred towards sin and love towards sinners, hatred towards Communism and love towards Communists. The reproach you made to me could be made to the Evangelists. Publishing what has been done to Jesus, they made people hate the Jews. Neither should the atrocities of Nazism be published. But those who think like you publish the unrighteousness committed by Ku-Klux-Klan and accuse southern authorities for alleged abuses against colored people, making so that these authorities should be hated. Only where the question comes to the Communists, here we must be delicate. What makes you favor them, if you are an anti-Communist as you say?

You said, I am wrong to call the Communists gangsters, although they have stolen whole countries. You said that not every Communist is a gangster. Neither was every Nazi a murderer, nor every Ku-Klux-Klan man. But Nazis are murderers. And Communists are gangsters. By violence and deceit they have conquered power and exercise it by terror everywhere. And you should fight against it, helping the oppressed Christians.

To this, you answered: "We have also taken away the country from the Indians." How can a Christian leader in such high position think so superficially? Suppose that a man would come to confess to you that he has two wives, would you say to him that it does not matter, because Abraham too had two wives? Since Abraham, many centuries have passed and we have evolved towards monogamy. What was tolerable then, is no more so today. When the Europeans took America from the Indians, there existed no international right yet, no declaration of the right of men, no organization of Allied Nations or League of Nations, no international conventions, etc. Phrases as yours are a defense of the aggressor. Tomorrow when the Chinese will throw the nuclear bomb upon America, you will say: "We also, centuries ago, have shot some Indians with guns. It is all right." Your thinking defends the Communist tyrants.

You said that to publish Communist atrocities will only strengthen American self-righteousness. Nobody who heard my preaching has this impression. But publishing of every crime and vice can have this result. We should not speak openly against drug-addictedness or drunkenness, because this will make the non-drunkards self-righteous. What logic is this? We have to speak against drunkenness and self-righteousness in the same time. So I do.

Next month, the patriarch Justinian of Rumania will be received with great honour by the World Council of Churches in Geneva. It will seem proud to you, but may I ask why such a reception has not been prepared to those who have suffered tortures for having worked on behalf of the World Council of Churches? We were not even asked what we eat, but you make reception to the Patriarch. What did he suffer for Christ's sake? I attended the election of Justinian as patriarch. Not one bishop voted for him, only the Communist laymen (in Roumania, then, the members of the Congress voted together with the bishops and the Congress was Communist). He has been made patriarch by the atheists, which constitutes the abomination of desolation. Afterwards he did what nearly all the Orthodox hierarchs do, he denounced priests and monks. I ask that, when he comes to Geneva, a commission should be named and I should prove before this commission my assertion.

Surely, the patriarch and the traitor Justin Moisescu, will also say something. They are masters in slandering. When Andre Gide, the French Communist writer, first wrote against Stalin, he was accused of homosexuality. When they quarrelled with Tito, they called him mass-murderer which was true, but also former paid agent of the Secret Police under the bourgeois regime, which had not been true. With us in Rumania, they killed Patrashcanu and put in prison Anna Pauker and Vasile Luca, their greatest leaders, accusing them that they had betrayed their comrades under the bourgeois regime to the Fascist Secret Police. Others they accused of adultery (they showed even faked pictures) and theft. They can invent many things. I don't know yet what they will invent about me.

I ask that neither I, nor they should be believed, but a trial should be made. The men whom you receive with honour in Geneva, who are they? They have put in prison a group of 400 farmers of "The Army of the Lord." They have put in prison all the nuns of the monastery Vladimireshti. They have put in prison their own priests. It is true that, whereas Justin Moisescu did it wholeheartedly, the patriarch did it reluctantly and then confessed to his confessor what he had done. But he did it. Seeing that he repented afterwards, I myself have considered him as my Christian brother. But afterwards he did it again and repented again, partly under my influence. We accepted him as brother again. Refusing to betray further, he was put aside and not allowed to come to the West. For whom knows things in the Communist camp, there is not the slightest doubt that the fact of his coming to the West now proves that he has yielded again and is again the tool of the Communists. He must be received with forgiving love and with concern to save his soul, not with honour as a Patriarch, and not as the leader of the real Orthodox church.

How much the tools of Communists can deceive is unimaginable. I know personally two cases when men came to priests and confessed with much contrition that they are working for the Secret Police. Now the priests had confidence in them, told them secrets and were betrayed. Never would the Patriarch be able to come out of the country and go back again, if the Communists would not be very sure that he will do their evil play abroad.

Now I am not against that even he should be received. But what do the Communists give in exchange? If you would have asked in exchange the right to create a Bible Society in Rumania, or something else, you would have obtained it. But we give everything, asking nothing.

In the hope that perhaps the agents of the Secret Police, who came as bishops to Geneva, will be converted, we take unconverted gangsters on the staff of the WWC, we make our decisions so that they should convene them and make the World Council of Churches be hated by thousands of Christians. I know many cases of Christians who left churches belonging to the W.C.C. because this favors the Communists. This is the loss of these churches. What do they gain in exchange, participating at this sinister comedy?

You told me that you cannot base your policy upon information given by refugees. So, when the Jews fled from Hitlerism, they were not reliable witnesses about the persecution! The Nazi should have been asked. The refugees represent the real church, the Underground Church.

I had a happy surprise when, as I mentioned the Underground Church, you said: "We, surely sustain the Underground Church." But I was quickly disappointed hearing that you sustain the Underground Church in... South Africa. May I know how many millions of Christians has Verwerd killed to make an Underground Church necessary there? But about Russia, they themselves have published that they have killed masses. So have they in all Communist countries. Should not be there an Underground Church? Should this not be sustained? And how can this be otherwise than by her refugees?

I am a little man, but I speak for those who cannot speak for themselves, for saints and martyrs who died in prison. It is their thoughts which I express. You cannot simply put aside what I say, relying on the information of those who have not suffered, have had no motive to flee and of whom some are traitors.

Night after night I have been interrogated about this World Council of Churches by the Communist Secret Police. I told you that the main purpose of this interrogatory was to see if I could not serve as their tool and if this World Council of Churches cannot be won for the Communist position. You were not interested to put me one question about this matter. How is it? Are you not prejudiced? Are you not afraid to hear the other side too? Political institutions asked me during hours about all the details of my interrogation and you did not put one question, because of the many "damned" lunches you have to eat, forgetting that in the Bible it is written that your table will be a snare for you. Fast three days and listen!

You not only asked nothing. I told you about Christians tied on crosses, upon the bodies of whom necessities were fulfilled, about priests obliged to say the holy mass over excrements and urine. Your only reaction was "Don't publish it." You had not a tear in your eyes. I have seen political leaders and innumerable rank and file Christians weeping when they heard about the martyrdom of their brethren. You do not feel with us. You do not weep with those who weep. Poor, poor soul! A religious leader in your position should be a man who inspires awe and you do not.

Before I left my fatherland, the Secret Police called me twice and said: "The dollars have been received by us. You will leave the country. Preach Christ as much as you like, but don't touch us, don't speak against us! (Approximately what you told me. Is it possible that you should be animated by the same spirit?) Otherwise for 1,000 dollars a gangster will kill you, we can bring you back (I have been in prison with men kidnapped from the West) or we can destroy you morally, inventing some story about you and the dupes in the West will believe it."

The men of the Communists are in Geneva and in the National Council of Churches. This letter will, probably, arrive also in their hands. A personality of the Lutheran World Federation told me that he had to destroy a cable which I sent to the World Council of Churches in Geneva in order that the Communists should not have it, so unsure is he about your staff. The reaction of the Communists will be violent. I know that I risk my life and reputation again, taking this position, but I owe it to the saints and heroes of the 20th century, who died near me for Christ. They asked it from those surviving.

I told you that I have a list of these saints, a list of 150 Protestant pastors recently deported to Siberia. How is it that you did not ask me for this list? Don't you intercede daily in prayer by name for the Christian martyrs? Then what else do you do? Would this not be a more profitable use of time than banqueting with Hromadkas and Justinians in Geneva and discovering new theologies, which are not the faith of our fathers, holy faith, for which even in this generation innumerable suffered and died?

You asked me that I should write to you practically what can be done. Now, many things are already done practically for the Church behind the Iron Curtain. But I cannot tell it to you who are involved in such friendship with the Communist world. It would mean to betray my brethren by neglect of the rules of conspiracy. I risk my life, not that of others. The only practical thing which I propose is that you should retire for a period in solitude with a good spiritual guide, passing time in prayer and fasting and find out the will of God. Once you will be nothing else than a poor sinner responding before the judgement of God for the support given to killers of Christians. Think about this! This is the most practical thing you can do.

But I would like to meet again in love with you and to speak about these things.

You are a very burdened man, you suffer much, you are like a beaten child; you have been trapped in a snare and don't know how to escape. Jesus loves you and asks you to return, to be on the side of martyrs and saints, not on the side of the oppressors. And so you may be sure of my love. I expect your answer.

Yours very sincerely,
R. Wurmbrand

Excerpts of a third letter to the same, 19th July, 1966

Dear Brother:

There is a verse in the Bible which I simply cannot fulfill. In I Timothy Ch. 5, V. 1 it is written, "Rebuke not an elder, but entreat him as a father". You have a more superior position in the Church than myself, who am an insignificant Pastor, and I would like to write to you entreatingly, as to a father, but I simply cannot, because the World Council of Churches, becomes more and more a channel of Communist propaganda.

I read the newspapers and cannot believe my eyes. At the World Conference of the World Council of Churches, Archpriest and traitor, Vitaly Borovoy, representative of the Moscow "Patriarchate of Clowns," said that he believed that the experience of the Russian Church showed that co-operation between Christianity and social revolutionists can take place. And there you were, and the American Bishops who praised Borovoy to me and Pastors, and did not protest.

I come from behind the Iron Curtain. I have led during many years secret Missionary work among the Russians, and can testify that Christianity has co-operated with the Communists as the hanged ones co-operate with the rope. 80,000 Orthodox Priests were killed physically. Communists wished to kill missions of Christians and Christians co-operated with them by giving their lives as sacrifices. Communists wished to torture and Christians co-operated, bearing tortures patiently. Communists wished to destroy thousands of Churches (from 1,000 Churches in pre-revolutionary Moscow only 40 were left), and Christians co-operated, agreeing to meet underground.

Communists poison our children with atheism, and Christians "co-operate" with them, weeping at this tragedy. Christian martyrs came home from prison and found their children Godless. Communists forbid the Bible (recently the Russians have stolen a car with Bibles which British Christians wished to smuggle in and "Trud", the Communist newspaper, wrote, "We will not allow our population to be poisoned by the Bible"), and Christians co-operate with them, writing the Bible by hand.

Speeches as that of Borovoy are delivered at the World Council of Churches, and this traitor is not driven out from the pulpit. His show-Church is not de-masked. This man, who praises the mass murderers of Christians, is on the staff of the World Council, but if American Christians knew of these crimes millions of them would refuse any support of the World Council.

The Communists torture and kill Christians, and you, by allowing such speeches, are partaking of the sins of the Communists.

It is only natural for the Communists to infiltrate the leadership of Church bodies. But where is the vigilance of Bishops? You breed at your bosom the serpent which will destroy the Church.

Yours very sincerely,
R. Wurmbrand

Excerpts of a fourth letter to the same

Dear Brother:

I received your letter of August 11, a letter which I admire for its politeness and humility. But I think that Christians should not avoid the way of the Cross. There exists a lifting up of the Cross also in exchange of letters.

You can speak politely, friendly, avoiding the main issues, and passing over deep spiritual conflicts with nice words. It was not the way of Jesus. Jesus had many qualities, but he had not very much the policy of politeness. He was invited to a dinner and said, being heard of those who had invited him, the purpose for which he had come: "I have come to call sinners to repentance." It is not very polite to call your host a sinner. In Luke II, beginning from verse 37, we read that the Pharisees invited him to dinner and the first words to the host were: "Fools, hypocrites", and with these polite words he left the house. Whosoever has read Luther knows that he never cared to be polite. The way of the peace of God is the way of spiritual struggle in which painful truths are said, but always out of love. I have the impression that many of the Christian leaders of the West avoid the Cross, not only in the life of the church and in the personal life, but even in the exchange of letters.

And therefore, I will not answer politely to your very polite letter. You leave without reply just the main subjects which I have put and therefore I repeat the questions. Is it right to make a bridge towards Communism with the risk of endangering the national security of America, as you, together with many others, declared?

Communism has just shown again its true face in the events of Red China for the admission of which in the Organization of the United Nations you have declared yourself. The events in China have shown that Communism means to be not only against God and against Christ but against Beethoven, Shakespeare, against pianos and against chess-play and against a boy kissing a girl. The Organization of the United Nations has a charter which Red China never respected, and the National Council of Churches instead of asking the expelling of all the other Communist countries from the Organization of the United Nations — asked that the Red Chinese barbarians should be received.

There is a practice now to say: "Well, the Chinese Communists are so bad, but the Russian and others are not." I can assure you that neither in Russia nor in Rumania you can buy in any bookshop a Bible or another religious book, nor can you buy Plato, Spinoza, Kant, Bergson or Einstein. You must never forget, that only a few months ago, Breshnev and Kosygin, as well as Ceausheseu, have declared, that the differences between the Russian and the Chinese Communism are slight. Should we endanger the national security of America for the sake of friendship with the foes, who endanger not Christianity only, but all civilizations, and even natural life? To this question you have to answer, and you have avoided it by polite words. And so with all the other questions raised in my previous letters.

You tell me, "I realize that what you write comes out of much suffering", which is again very nice, but I, very unpolitely ask the question what have you done to the alleviating of this suffering?

How much has the World Council of Churches given for the families of Christian martyrs in Rumania and Russia? They do not even know the names of these martyrs. I ask you, dear Brother, what value has your polite phrase: "I realize that what you write comes out of much suffering", when you do nothing to make it more bearable?

When are you decided to meet me and other representatives of the suffering Underground Church in order to work out the practical means of alleviating its suffering? Phrases, only phrases — or as Jesus would put it. leaves, leaves — without fruits!

You say secondly that the World Council of Churches stands in opposition to all kinds of persecution, whether on grounds of race, religion or political views. It is not true. Against apartheid in South Africa you declare yourself, telling the name of the guilty. You accused Rhodesia for its alleged unjust attitude towards the colored population. You take a firm stand against any racial discrimination in the States. In the decision of the World Council of Churches against anti-Semitism, you did not say that Communist countries are the only ones in which anti-Semitism is the official policy. Russia is taboo, nothing should be said against it. Did the World Council of Churches at its last sitting protest against the crime of genocide, committed by the Chinese government against the Tibetan people? Has the World Council of Churches protested against the fact that the Catholics are persecuted in Poland, that the Orthodox personality David Balauta has recently been sentenced in Rumania because he spoke about Christ to a few children? Has it protested against the fact that Baptist pastors are imprisoned in Russia? On the contrary: archpriest and archtraitor Borovoy and his boss, the archbishop Nikodem, gave Russia as an example of friendly co-operation between Christianity and the social revolution. In Indonesia, hundreds of thousands of Communists have been killed in the last upheaval; they have been killed and tortured without judgement. The World Council of Churches did not protest. The Russians liked the killing of Indonesian Communists, because those were on the side of the Chinese. And whatever pleases the Russian Bolshevists, pleases the World Council of Churches too. The World Council of Churches has not shown the slightest opposition to this mass-murdering of unjudged men. So you pronounce yourselves against any persecution only when it happens in the Capitalist World. For the Russian Communists everything is allowed. Moscow government is represented in Geneva and dominates there by its pseudo-bishops.

You write: "The World Council of Churches has to find the ways in which it can best help those in persecution." I repeat, those persecuted by the Communist states, Christians, Jews, Moslems, Buddhists, Socialists, and opponent Communists, have never been helped by the World Council of Churches, and never has even a word of sympathy been expressed towards them. You may say that it is difficult to do it for them who are behind the Iron Curtain. I can assure you that neither have martyrs who came to the West, after years in Communist prison received even a word of warm welcome in the West or a letter of Christian love.

You object against what you call my basic opinion "that only those who are persecuted are true to the faith". In this question I have nothing to answer to you. Your debate is with Jesus Christ who says in Luke 9:23 that "If any one wishes to be a follower of mine ... day after day he must take up his cross and follow me." When you will meet Jesus, you will be able to tell Him that He was wrong, as you tell me that you cannot accept that only those who are persecuted are true to faith. Wherever militant and persecuting atheism dominates, you have to be either a collaborator or the persecuted one, and only the latter is true to his faith.

You call the official leaders of the Churches behind the Iron Curtain "alleged collaborators." What would you say, if I would call the Ku-Klux-Klan "alleged racists" and the Nazis "alleged killers of Jews"? It is self-understood that in a country where there is no political liberty, in which even a Communist is killed by his comrades, if he sustains his party line to only 99%, religious liberty cannot exist. Communism can exist only by terror. It has to put in prison even a Mihailoff, because it is anti-human and contradicts life. If religious leaders have liberty under such a regime, if they have liberty even to come to Geneva (when we were beaten for having passed from one prison cell to the other), then it is sure that they have supports and empowerment of the tyrants.

If you will know that somebody tries to deceive a girl of yours, who is naive, you would warn her. And so the Underground Church from behind the Iron Curtain has charged me to warn the Western Christians against those known by us to be traitors.

The Underground Church has its members in the Communist Secret Police, in the official Church and even in the World Council of Churches. These surely will never be known by you, and through them we know things which you cannot know. We know that not only the Orthodox bishops who come to Geneva are collaborators with the Communists, but we know by name also the Western religious leaders who play the same ugly role of helping the mass-killers of Christians to dominate the world.

Dear brother, you may be sure that I will never cease to love you and to pray for you, and that my harsh words come from a loving heart.

Yours very sincerely,
Richard Wurmbrand

To another of the leaders of the World Council of Churches
and Lutheran World Federation:

Dear Brother:

I was honored to make your acquaintance. The problem which we discussed was too important to leave without further elaboration. For that reason I write to you.

You mentioned the name of a Russian priest, one whom you believed to be a sincere representative of the Russian Orthodox Church and who is sent by the Russian Church to Geneva.

Now I would like to share something of my personal experience. No Westerner can understand how the Communists work, and what masters they are in dressing things up in false clothing . . .

Trotsky has been slain by an agent of Stalin who played perfectly his role of being a Trotskyist. He first won the confidence of Trotsky, a man who was not naive. Then one day he killed him with a blow of a hammer upon his head.

It is utterly inconsistent that the Russian or Rumanian Orthodox clergymen should have the possibility of coming to Geneva and returning without reporting on their total activity and on his extra contacts. Every clergyman should read the Penkovsky papers. Penkovsky was a colonel of the Russian secret police. As such he did spy work in England. The authenticity of these papers is unquestionable. In those he attests to the fact that the Russian police are being served by Bishops and Priests.

I am all for accepting these representatives at Geneva. Jesus did not reject anyone, so Geneva should reject no one, but should strive to bring them to repentance. Only they should not be allowed to participate in the actions and the program planning of the church.

In every business transaction both parties must share. I give you the clothes. You give me the money. We accept the Russian agents in Geneva. Have we ever asked for something in exchange? Have we, for example ever asked permission to establish a Bible Society in Rumania? We accept from the Communists and we ask nothing in exchange. Their spies are allowed to come to Geneva and return freely. We are not allowed to go to Moscow and Bucharest and represent the Gospel of Christ.

In every period of the Church, we have to concentrate on principles involved. Thus the issue of the menace of Communism to Christianity must be reckoned with. You told me that you consider that the most serious menace to Christianity today is the affluence and the intellectualism of the world. However it might be well to remember the Latin saying, "First you must live. Afterward you make philosophy". Americans give to Christians and Christianity the possibility to live. Russians uproot both Christians and Christianity.

In a certain fellowship each one was asked what book he would most desire to take with him if he were to leave a sinking ship. One answered that he would take with him a work of Shakespeare; another answered that he would take the Bible. The right answer given by one was: I desire to take a book that would teach me how to build a boat so that I might escape from an isolated island where I might be stranded, and might find a place where I could choose the books I desired to have access to. The first need is for liberty. Every dictatorship disposes of men by making it impossible for him to live in an atmosphere of truth. America seeks to foster freedom so that men might find truth.

I have known Rumanians who have suffered and died for having expressed sympathy with America. They were willing to suffer these things because a country like America was to them a symbol of freedom to worship as they desired. For this reason Americans should strive to understand the responsibility which is placed upon their shoulders. They must keep a sensitive conscience for the responsibility to fight Communism.

It is often charged that Americans have also been responsible for cruelties and tyrannies. Reference is made to oppression of the Negroes in the South, or atrocities by American soldiers in Viet Nam. Surely America as a whole continent has both its saints and its criminals. But America does not seek to promote criminals. With the Communists, violence, cruelty, and atheism are an essential part of the doctrine. Some American personalities have spread the opinion that there exist different kinds of Communism. They contrast Stalinist Communism with that found in Yugoslavia. If they had lived under this "good Yugoslavian Communism" they would have found that they had no right to say a word of criticism against Tito.

It is impossible to exaggerate concerning what the Communists have done to the Christian Church. At the time of the Russian revolution in 1917, Russia had 100,000 Orthodox priests. Nearly 45,000 of these have been killed. The Catholic Church has also been destroyed gradually. No one can know how many bishops, priests, nuns and monks have been killed in Rumania. The same is true in Hungary and Bulgaria; many people have also been put to death.

You told me the story of an East German bishop, who after many interventions obtained the right to make a Christian home for aged men. I can tell you similar stories from Rumania. Only your conclusion that we can obtain from the Communists by persistent intervention important concessions is wrong.

Shepherds have told me that when wolves enter their flocks, they never steal old sheep. They only go for the lambs. The Communists do the same. They want our youth between the ages of 18 and 19. They do not mind that we establish homes for the aged. But where are the lambs? Christian education for children in Communistic countries can only be offered underground. Any bishop who does not organize such an underground ministry is not a good bishop, even if he organizes homes for the aged.

I was very disturbed to hear that the next conference of the Lutheran World Federation is to be held in Eastern Germany. Suppose that I or someone else in my situation should be chosen to be a delegate to this conference, surely we could not go there. I have been in a Rumanian prison with men who have been kidnapped from Germany.

Not all Lutheran leaders in Communist countries have made compromises. But some have remained silent. The real Church dare not remain silent. The true men and women of God who suffer for the name of Jesus behind the Iron Curtain ought to have a right to expect the sympathy and moral support of the rest of the Church. This has not been forthcoming, and all the while others have been represented at Geneva. I myself have been told by the Lutheran World Federation not to come to Geneva because the Communists would know of it.

I have the list of 150 Protestant pastors recently deported to Siberia. Never has anyone in Geneva asked me for this list. I would have thought that they would have been interested in this. First of all, it was their duty to pray for these men. Secondly, if they would have asked me, I would have shown them the possibility of bringing help secretly to the families of these men who are in jail behind the Iron Curtain. I was asked about my health. Never was I asked for this list. This is wrong!

God sends His rain upon the just and the unjust. I agree that love must be extended to Communists as well as Christians. What of the fact that there have been from the leaders of the World Council of Churches words of sympathy only for the Communists, but never for the suffering brethren who serve as faithful brethren behind the Iron Curtain? Their families have not felt the brotherly love of the Lutheran World Federation and of the World Council of Churches.

I apologize if some things I have told you are disturbing.

I remain most sincerely,
Richard Wurmbrand

A second letter to the same

Dear Brother:

I risk to become annoying by my letters, I know. But the questions mentioned in our last discussion were much too important and through me speak those who usually have no possibility to speak themselves, being muzzled by the Communists. No representative from Geneva can speak in the East with the Underground Church. We have also faithful bishops in the East, but "bishop XY" told me that he discovered a microphone in his table, at which he had spoken with foreign delegates. So even the best have to be very careful there.

I don't agree with you that Communism is not wrong in itself. A Communism in itself does not exist. Communism has to be put in practice. When you put it in practice, you see that it contradicts human nature. Even a dog wishes to possess a bone of his own. Communism wishes to take from everybody everything. In the Communist Manifesto of Karl Marx, the basic document of Communism, it is clearly stated that the last aim is also the communization of women. Such a program can be put in practice only by terror. And to jusitfy the terror, you have to uproot religions which preach love and goodness. Barbarity and atheism are undissolubly connected with Communism. Every philosophical concession to an abstract Communist principle serves the Communist propaganda. Jesus warned us that wolves will come in skins of sheep. Communists dress their barbarity in beautiful words. And if I say simply "Oh, their words are beautiful" without adding immediately: "but these words are lies in the mouth of the Communists, their aims being bad", I help them to deceive the sheep over which I am put as shepherd. Let us judge after the fruits, after the reality, not after beautiful phrases! I will never say one good word about the killers of my brethren.

If I understand right, you said that it is not my business to speak against the Communist governments. When I left Rumania, the Secret Police told me: "Preach Christ, only don't touch us." But Christ cannot be preached, I cannot teach the sheep, without telling them openly what you have told me, that Communism is devilish, demoniac. It is part of our prophetic office to speak against the beasts. So did the prophets of old. No one who does not condemn decidedly the unrighteouness, cruelty and atheism of the Communist rulers is accepted by our oppressed peoples as teacher in religion. We have to do this part, too. We learned it from Luther.

As Niemoeller and Bonhoeffer were anti-Hitlerians and did not preach an abstract Gospel, so we must do against Communism too. Niemoeller and Bonhoeffer were condemned in their time by many bishops. When Communism will be overthrown, surely, everybody will say that I have been right. We must not wait until then, but be the protagonists of the anti-Communist faith. This without making of anti-Communism a new Gospel, as some may do, who defend against Communism their bank accounts and not Christ. Christ is our message and part of this message is opposition to Communism.

You said that we have to accept the representatives chosen by the Eastern churches. Chosen by whom? I attended the last Baptist congress in Bucharest. The official candidates for leadership got only nine votes. One of them stood up and said: "We have to be chosen". They were rejected again. At the third election they were "chosen", without any contracandidate. So it happens in all religions. The delegates of the East do not represent the church (with a few exceptions of very good men, but who had also to compromise). They wished to make of me a bishop and I know what conditions they put me. If I would have accepted them, I would have to come to Geneva as representative, but I would not have said the truth. Now these delegates, who represent the Communist beast, participate at taking resolutions and all resolutions are made so that they should be acceptable to these bishops, who represent the demonical power.

The Western Christians know it. Innumerable Christians and Pastors with whom I spoke in the West are sad about it. I remember to have met only once one man who approves it.

I am against the resolution taken by the World Council of Churches in the Vietnam-question. Opposition to Communism must be shown in the resolutions of the World Council of Churches. It must be said that we have it to do with arch-liars. They cannot be put on the same level as Americans, inviting both parts to make peace. We disarm by this only the West.

Anti-Communism must be as decided as anti-Hitlerism was in the hearts of the faithful.

Yours very sincerely,
Richard Wurmbrand

Excerpts of a third letter to the same

Dear Brother:

I received your letter of the 1st July.

Since I wrote you last, a new ignominy happened. Four young Christians tried to fulfill their Christian duty and to smuggle in Bibles in a country in which millions hunger after the Word of God and don't get it. The Russians, who stole half of Europe, stole also the Bibles and the car. They may need it for transporting Christian prisoners from one jail to the other.

Dr. XY, (Dr. in I don't know what, but in Christianity in no case,) one of the leaders of the British Baptist Union and one of the leading personalities of the World Council of Churches immediately declared publicly that his Union has nothing to do with it and that he observes carefully the Soviet regulations, which forbid to give the Word of God to hungry souls. I expected that the next day you will publish a declaration asking that this man should be expelled from the World Council of Churches.

Just recently the bolshevik Patriarch Justinian has been received with honour in Geneva. The World Council of Churches has published high praises about the religious liberty in the Soviet camp (read the January issue of the International Review of Missions). Archbishop Nikodem also publishes the religious liberty in Russia and nobody demasked on the spot his lies. Now the Soviet Government itself slaps its supporters. The Soviet newspaper, "Trud" publishes that they will never allow the poison of the Bible to enter in Russia. I expected that on the next day the World Council of Churches will take a resolution of protest, as it has taken in the cases of South Africa, Rhodesia and so on. Must only colored men not be persecuted? White men can be persecuted for their faith! I warned you that the Soviet Agents with beards lie. Now you have the proof.

The British Bible Society in whose museum I saw how it boasts with the Bibles printed secretly by Tyndale and others in times before, also published immediately a declaration assuring everybody that they had nothing to do with this action, as if it would be a crime.

To remain silent when such ignominies happen is to become accomplice with those who confiscate Bibles. The foreigners have been expelled. We have private information that the Russian brethren connected with this are put in prison. I have known the Russian brethren. They bear such things gladly. But who takes their defense?

Leaders of the Lutheran World Federation spoke with the authorities of Eastern Germany, authorities of the bandit Ulbricht which no civilized Government recognizes, about arranging the future conference of the Lutheran World Federation in Weimar, (East Germany). Then the American Ambassador in Bonn asked you: "Have you asked Washington about it?" You answered as it suits a church leader in a free country: "Since when have we to ask Washington about what we do?" Very fine! A church leader should not ask Washington. But should he ask the usurpatory Government of a dictatorial Communist country? If he does so, why not rather the freely chosen authorities of his own fatherland? All these things are very strange to me, and to innumerable rank and file Christians and pastors.

In the beginning, the Roman bishop has been considered as the senior bishop, because Rome gave in the first centuries the most martyrs. Those who have the most to say in the universal church today are the martyrs of the Underground Church behind the Iron Curtain, not the Popes, neither those who lead an easy life in the West. And I speak in the name of the Underground Church in the leadership of which I have been for years. What they say has the most weight, because they have given blood for what they say. By secret channels I receive letters from them. They are scandalized by the complacency of Western church leaders with their persecutors.

Do you think that the National Council of Churches confuses the fight for civil rights with the proclamation of the Gospel? Do you think that the World Council of Churches confuses the fight for the emancipation of the black people in Africa with the proclamation of the Gospel? Why do you suppose that I confuse the fight against the mass-killers and torturers of Christians (this is the explanation of the word Communist) with the proclamation of the Gospel? Favorable letters from your pastors and laymen, which you can get, tell that my sermons gave them the possibility to say, "Now we have seen Jesus" and that I brought Pentecost in their Church. You are the only one who expresses fear.

I risk daily my life to give to the Communists the best I have: the Gospel.

Yesterday a Christian leader told me: "Preach only Christ and don't preach against Communism." I said "Were Niemoeller, Bonhoeffer and the others right not to preach only Christ, but to take a stand against Hitlerism?" He answered: "Surely yes, seeing that Hitler killed 6 millions of Jews." I said again: "But Communists have killed 30 millions of Russians and millions of Chinese. Why is it not right to take energetically a stand against them?" His answer was: "You are mad."

I propose the following:

1. The World Council of Churches should protest immediately with the

Soviet and the other Communist governments, giving the list of Christian prisoners and asking that these men should be immediately released and compensated for their unjust detention.

2. The World Council of Churches should ask the American and other Governments to protest at the Organization of the United Nations against the lack of religious liberty in the Soviet Camp.

3. As these men have been denounced by the leaders of the Baptist Union, who are Communist agents, the World Council of Churches should ask immediately free elections of the leadership of religious bodies.

4. The World Council of Churches should put in view to Archbishop Nikodim, Borovoi and all the other Soviet agents in Geneva that they will be expelled from the World Council of Churches, if our Christian brethren are not released immediately.

5. The World Council of Churches should demand immediately that the Communist countries should keep the liberties to which they have pledged themselves in accepting the charter of the OUN. She should ask immediately for the right to open in every Communist Country:

(a) an office of the World Council of Churches

(b) a Bible society

(c) a YMCA

(d) Sunday schools for children

(e) free religious press

Otherwise the Russian and other churches cannot remain on the World Council of Churches, seeing that they do not represent the real Church, but the Soviet Secret Police.

6. The World Council of Churches should ask the right to visit and send parcels to those who are in prison for religious motives. Until obtaining this right, the World Council of Churches should organize the immediate secret relief of the prisoners and their families. About this I could give advice.

7. The World Council of Churches should organize a direct missionary work behind the Iron Curtain.

I guarantee that 90% of the members of your church would agree with the content of this my letter and my demands. They would be scandalized to know that their contributions go towards dining men like Archbishop Nikodim and Patriarch Justinian (men of the Communists) while families of Christian martyrs in Russia and Rumania never received one cent, although they were the most entitled.

The publishing of these facts would have as result a great revolt among the church members and massive leavings of the church, which must be avoided by all means. I love the churches which some in America have begun to hate. I love the church leaders too, even those who are wrong. But the scandal cannot continue. What I ask above is the demand of the whole Underground Church in the Soviet camp. I can speak in its name. I represent them, and I ask in their name.

We have information that the Communists are preparing a subtle campaign of denigrating me, using for this, their tools in the church. We ask you to be on our side.

I have been in the States only three months. Already many couriers have been sent to the Soviet camp with relief for families of martyrs. How much more could you do this in your position. Of the couriers sent by us, never has anybody been caught.

Just because I love you so much and appreciate you highly, I write to you so plainly what I have on my bleeding heart. I don't know how you sleep the nights. It is very late in the night now. I cannot sleep with the thought of those who suffer in the third part of the world and with the thought of leaders of the World Council of Churches who sympathize with the oppressed.

Yours very sincerely,

R. Wurmbrand

Excerpt of a fourth letter to the same

Dear Brother:

Somebody who is close to you asked a friend of mine to "take Wurmbrand off your back". In your last letter a note of irritation was detectable. So I assure you that this will be the last private letter you will receive from me, unless you express the desire to continue the correspondence with me.

I find it understandable that my letters are irritating to you and to your

friends. Many things seem to irritate you, as for example the war fought by
the Americans in Vietnam. But the fact that millions of Christians have been
and are tortured and killed in the Soviet area does not seem to irritate you!
I see this from the fact that at the last sitting of the World Council of Churches
a decision was taken against the war in Vietnam and a cable was sent to
President Johnson. President Johnson may defend himself and the war. It is not
my business. But I would have expected the World Council of Churches also
to send cable to Brejnev and Mao-Tse-Tung and Causchescu asking them to
stop torturing your brethren in faith! Supposing that the fight in Vietnam is
an injustice, is it the only one? Is not the killing of Christians an equal injustice?

The leaders of the World Council of Churches sat there while Borovoy and
the Archbishop Nikodem praised Communism and held forth Russia as an
example of cooperation between Christians and the atheist Communist revolution. They had nothing to say. Did they not know that the Communist revolution
began with the putting in prison of Patriarch Tihon? Did they not know that
the Catholic and Lutheran Churches in Russia have been uprooted? Can it
be that you are unacquainted with what the Communists themselves have
published about the killing of millions of Christians by Stalin, while Mikoyan,
Brejnev and Kosygin were his executioners? Do you not know that they are
poisoning the whole youth with atheism, not permitting the Christians to re-
spond? One is entitled to presume that the Church leaders are as well informed
as the average layman. The above is today general knowledge. And still one
lends one's ears to claims of cooperation between Christianity and an atheist
inspired ideology — Communism!

Not one protested against Borovoy. An American leader of the World Council kissed the Archbishop Nikodem.

At the Council of Nicea, St. Nikolas slapped the heretic Arius and legend
tells that the holy Virgin descended visibly from heaven to crown him for this.
Today we recite the Nicean creed, but only the words are spoken; we no
longer have the spirit of those who composed it. We kiss those who are worse
than Arius.

No civilized state recognizes the bandit Ulbricht. Leaders of the Lutheran
World Federation conferred with the mass-killer Ulbricht's authorities in order
to organize the conference of the Lutheran World Federation in Eastern Germany. They, the Ulbrichts, accepted this honour shown them in their cus-
tomary manner. They snubbed you with words which would be something
like the following: "We have attained our purpose. We have been recognized

by American Christians in spite of their Government. The Lutheran World Federation has made proposals to us asking of us favours. Thus, we no longer need you. Hold your Congress somewhere else! We are so certain that you will still praise us and we need not waste time and expense by receiving you in our country."

I am asked in your letter why it is that I fail to appreciate that a Mission behind the Iron Curtain is not one which can be created at once, as I propose. But when have I proposed it should be done quickly? Bolshevism has been in power for 50 years in Russia. Did the American churches have to wait 50 years for Wurmbrand to come and tell them their missionary duty to preach Christ is an atheist Bolshevik country?

Has Christ placed any boundaries where His gospel is to be preached? Is it not to be preached to all men? Did the Bolsheviks cease to be men? Do they not also have souls to be saved?

No, Wurmbrand does not come to tell you to begin new tasks. He reproves you for having neglected your duty for 50 years. And for this it is, he says, that not another day can be lost. Your neglect has led to the loss of millions of souls. Because of this, all else must be put aside. You can put aside fraternization with Communists in Geneva and instead convene all presidents to fly in the next day and to make restitutions for what has been neglected.

Instead you use time for leaders of the World Council of Churches to come to Geneva and to vote a resolution in which they declare violence as justified in certain cases.

They then cable to President Johnson that his anti-communist violence is not justifiable. What violence is this that you speak of as justifiable? Only the Communist one? Against this you had not a word to say.

Now our ways part. On my side, I will go another way, without the slightest bitterness against you, but I must tell you that by fraternizing with the Communists at the World Council of Churches you share also the sins of the Communists, who murder millions of souls with their atheistic poison and their persecution. The more loving I am towards you personally, the more I suffer grief at the tragic part you play.

In order to help man to be righteous before God — which is the greatest service one man can do towards another — one must at times be harsh. If I am harsh, you must believe my motives.

And so the voice declared to be prophetic in a letter of a big denomination of America is treated as Priests have always treated prophets. You have not listened to him and you have driven him out.

Be sure, you will never cease to be in my prayers and in my love.

Yours very sincerely,

R. Wurmbrand

Post Scriptum

I wonder about the lack of harshness in my letters. Recently we got the news: A Rumanian Orthodox leader had been put in prison 7 years ago, leaving a family with 6 children. The wife was sick. The two elder daughters could get no jobs, being daughters of a counter-revolutionary. But there were 4 smaller children to feed. So the daughters of the Christian martyr, Christians themselves, prostituted themselves to support their family. The brother, aged 14, seeing his sisters becoming harlots, became mad. When the arrested brother came home after amnesty, he found this tragedy and wished only one thing, to go back to prison and not to see anymore this dark picture. His wish has been fulfilled. Recently he has been rearrested for renewed Christian activity. Will I ever be harsh and stern enough with you? Will ever God forgive me any polite word, when daughters of Christian martyrs are harlots to sustain their families?

Excerpts from another letter to the same

Dear Brother:

To Mrs. H.... you wrote that she is wrong to base only on information from one part. From how many parts have you information? Have you the slightest connection with the Underground Church behind the Iron Curtain? Do you ask this Church too? I know five men from the Underground Church of different Communist countries who are in the West now. Why are they not asked? How is it that the World Council of Churches invites only the collaborators of the Communist regime and never gave a hearing to martyrs? They would have had to tell you very interesting things.

The main goal of my interrogation was not about what we have done, but about how the World Council of Churches can be used for Communist purposes. Would it not have been interesting for the World Council of Churches to know the details of such interrogations? How is it that political institutions of America were more interested to know things than the American leaders of the World Council of Churches?

Is it not a shame that neither the rich Church of England, nor the American churches have a yearly special budget for relief to families of Christian martyrs, when they know that in a third of the world the Christians are oppressed? If in Red China, men are beaten with ropes on the streets, imagine what happens to Christians in a Chinese jail!

For the admission of Red China in the United Nations, there were precise resolutions of Council of Churches and from church-leaders. Why did not these councils gather to protest against the terror in Red China and to inquire how the Christians there can be helped?

I hope that you will intervene immediately! The Lutheran World Federation, and the World Council of Churches should have a regular budget for relief to families of Christian martyrs (curtailing eventually for this purpose, if there is no other source of income, the salaries of their workers), that the Underground Church should be represented in these bodies, that its representatives and martyrs should be heard with the due respect. They are not beggars with whom you can finish by giving them a few dollars. They are the worthiest part of the universal church, who have conquered by sacrifices of liberty and life the right to be listened to.

Otherwise no blessing can come on these institutions from God.

Yours,
R. Wurmbrand

Excerpts from another letter to same

Dear Brother:

You hide wrong attitudes under beautiful phrases like: "We must not judge the situation in the East after Western standards." Would it be right to say: "We must not judge gangsters after the standards of the honest world"? The world of tyranny must be called so and you who take a clear stand against racial discrimination in the States, should take the same firm stand against the religious persecution in the East.

What would you say about a Lutheran who is a Catholic? You would say that it is nonsense. But you say that you have known faithful Christians who are members of the Communist Party, which is avowedly atheistic. You should have rather praised the innumerable Christians I have known, who preferred to die than to become members of an atheistic party. My son refused at the age of 10 to wear the red necktie and to be a member of the Communist children-organization. He was thrice driven out from school for this. And he was not the only one. The praise of these should be in the mouth of a church leader.

Yours very sincerely,

R. Wurmbrand

Excerpts from another letter to the same

Dear Brother:

When you are beaten at the bottom of the feet, you cry in a very unreasonable manner. And when you continue to feel to be one body with those beaten like this in the Communist camp, you simply cry and others dismiss you as unmannered.

Did you hear as I do about what happens to the bodies of the imprisoned Chinese Christians? The Red Guards have cut off the ears, the tongues and legs of Church leaders and other Christians who did not wish to deny Christ. They have put nuns to trample on crosses. One of them died of abuses. And at once the great Christian bodies who asked with great noise for the admission of Red China in the OUN, although it does not respect the charter of this organization, have become silent. Why are they not noisy now? Why don't they protest loudly?

There is a chasm between those who have passed through the ordeal of Communist prisons and those who have not passed. Nobody can pass over this chasm from either side. We hear day and night the cries of those tortured and feel their tortures as ours, as is ordered by God in Hebr. 13.3, and behave with great cries. We will never understand those who remain silent. We wonder about each other.

Let us judge as things are judged before every human court: by witnesses.

Would you like that we should organize a show-trial of the churches behind the Iron Curtain? We could bring there Father Grigore, a Catholic priest, who has published "Through God's Underground". He has been for years under disguises and nicknames in the Communist countries and speaks about the Protestant Underground. Read Father Czisak's "With God in Russia", again a Catholic priest, who met in Russian prisons Communists who had prepared themselves in theological seminaries to become Orthodox bishops. Read the firsthand book "Come Wind, Come Weather" by Leslie Lyall, about the bankruptcy of the official church-leaders in Red China. Read the surely genuine Penkovsky papers. They are written by a Colonel of the Russian Secret Police, who gave his life for liberty. He asserts that all the Official church-leaders in Russia are their agents.

How could you be intimately acquainted with them? You have spoken with them for hours either in their country, where they feared the microphones or in the West, where they feared that any indiscretion by the one to whom they confide themselves may mean their death. We know them from years of work.

I would ask you: Was Bishop Berggrav of Norway right to take public attitude against Nazism, when the Germans stole his country? If yes, are the Baltic bishops right who say not a word against the Russians who have stolen theirs, but the more praise the Soviet regime? Either Berggrav was wrong in what he did or the Baltic bishops are wrong, not doing the same thing. Were Niemoeller and Bonhoeffer and the others right in taking attitude against Nazism, although this meant for them prison and death? If yes, are the Lutheran bishops in the East right, who not one takes open attitude against Bolshevism? Hitler has killed 6 millions of Jews and had to be fought against. The Communists have killed 30 million Russians. Of 1000 churches of Moscow, 40 have remained. They have killed millions in all countries. Why do we praise those who have taken an open stand against Hitlerism and don't expect that the same attitude should be taken against Communism too?

Not one Protestant bishop of the East has done it. Otherwise he would have been in prison. The Catholic bishops in Rumania have done it without exception. Nearly all died under tortures in prison. Were they stupid to do so? Or will they be those crowned by God as martyrs? Then the others must be wrong.

The Protestant bishops of the East are accomplices of Communism, at least by their silence.

But what to say about Bishop Dezsery of Hungary who came to Rumania to teach us to substructurate theologically Communism? Thousands have heard him preaching. What about Bishop Veto, whose articles denouncing Ordass as counterrevolutionary appeared in his periodical? What about bishop-vicar Rapp of Rumania, whom everybody knows as denouncer and who teaches that God has given three revelations: through Moses, Jesus and Marx?

Bishop XY is my friend, but he too is wrong and I told it to him often. He is since years member of the Communist Parliament. In this time, laws giving death sentence for trifles were made, laws restricting religious liberty, laws by which farmers and barbers were expropriated of their land and of their shops, laws of atheistic education. If he would have voted against or would have said one word, he would have gone to prison. And everybody wonders why he has not chosen this. Don't you take the responsibility of a body if you belong to it and say no word of protest?

Excerpts from another letter to the same leader of the
World Council of Churches
Dear Brother:

You say: Wurmbrand is a martyr, a prophetic voice needed by the church. But the church should remain without the so rare prophetic voice and without the advice of a martyr. You say that you and others cannot recommend to your congregations the one man you declare to be a martyr and a prophetic voice.

How is this possible?

You give some explanations, but say that there are others more extreme which you do not wish to repeat.

I will tell these extreme things:

I accuse you and the other Western leaders of the World Council of Churches to have brought the wolf in the stable of the sheep, with the result that the sheep will be destroyed.

You have brought into the World Council of Churches the Orthodox hierarchy from the Communist countries, explaining that we must understand them, they being Christians in the atheist Communist society, who have had "to make some adjustments". (Arizona Daily Star, 2.11.1963)

Now listen to the adjustments and who these wolves are in the hands of whom you have given the flock. I quote from the Journal of the Moscow Patriarchate, from articles of the Metropolitan Nikolaie of Leningrad, whom you have received with great honours, as a Christian brother, to America:

"America, that fornicatrix of the resurrected Babylon, having arranged a world market, attempts to seduce peoples, pushing them on to war"... Its freedom is "freedom to rob, to do violence, to kill — this is their freedom." "The United States are the beast of Apocalypse." Continuing, he describes the actions of Americans "Cynically violated standards not only of international rights, but of human morals. Executions without trial and inquisitions, secret and public. Dreadful tortures of victims. The cutting off of ears and noses, breasts, putting out of eyes, etc. The Americans are civilized savages".

I would consider every man who fraternizes with somebody who saith such things against my fatherland and my nation as guilty of high treason.

Is this "an adjustment"? Neither Stalin, nor Khruschev have ever said such criminal things against American Christians what Metropolitan Nikolaie said. Here just another phrase of his: "The great blasphemy from the Christian point of view, is the fact that these people call themselves Christians."

Archbishop Nikodem of Russia is of the same type. He declared at the last session of the World Council of Churches that he entirely agrees with the politic of the Soviet Government. This has recently arrested hundreds of Baptists. Many died because of the tortures. I keep the lists of the arrested ones and the proofs of the tortures to the disposition of everyone who wishes to have them. Radio Moscow announced the sentencing of Christians for the crime of having poisoned children with Christian teachings. I possess the picture of the trial and can show it to anyone. The Soviets published recently new laws punishing with 3-5 years of prison those who teach children about Christ or will multiply religious literature. With this politic Archbishop Nikodem entirely agrees. And you entirely agree with Nikodem and recognize this bandit as a bishop.

The more so: "The Ecumenical Press Service" No. 17/66 praised these anti-Christian laws for an example of the easing of earlier laws about religion, which had the result that, on the 30th August, 1966, in "Izvestia," the official organ of the mass-murderers and torturers of Christians, which call themselves Soviet-Government, Kuroiedov, the head of the Department of Cults, the one who heads the liquidation of religion, greatly praises the World Council of

Churches. I would blush if such a murderer of Christians would praise me. I would step out of any organization praised by the mass-murderers of Christians.

Nikolaie and Nikodim are decorated by the Soviet-Government. So are the Rumanian Lutheran bishops. Would you have accepted in wartime decorations from Hitler? The Communists have imposed themselves upon our countries by deceit and terror. Never has any nation chosen by free elections a Communist Government. Everywhere they have killed and tortured. The Lutheran Church of Bucharest where I served before has been transformed in a cinema. And the bishops with whom you collaborate and which you defend not to be stooges are decorated by these worst enemies of Christianity. Why?

The Communists have published that Stalin has been a mass-murderer. Mikoyan has been his right hand. And Hromadka highly praised Mikoyan. And murderer Mikoyan highly praised Hromadka and the World Council of Churches.

These are the extreme things which you hid in your circular letter. I am sure that no president, no pastor and no laymen with Christian and patriotic feelings will agree with your embracing and bringing in the World Council of Churches these foes. About Metropolitan Nikolaie, an official document issued by the Committee of Internal Security of your Senate states that he is an agent of the Communist Secret Police. These are those with whom you collaborate and whom you have recognized as leaders of the Universal Church. Opening the churches for them, it was only natural that you had to close them for the one whom you call a martyr and the prophetic voice. Who opens the church for Judas, has to close it for those who — as you say — have suffered for the truth.

This is the essence of our conflict, which you have passed by invoking childish pretexts.

I told you three things which you should have known without me. First, that Jesus has said "Go and teach all nations", not all the nations until the Iron Curtain. Why has your Church no mission to the Communist world, although this exists since 50 years? You give the explanation in your letter. You do "what the law will allow". Which law? The American laws don't hinder me in such a work. It is the law of the Communists. And you consider as your duty to respect this law. If the Christians of the first centuries would have respected the laws of the Roman Empire and Luther the laws of the Pope, where would we have been? The first Christians worked secretly and so must we not caring at all about the laws of mass-murderers of Christians and mass-poisoners of children and youth.

I told you that the most real church behind the Iron Curtain is the one led by the underground leaders and that we must join hands with her. I told you that the families of Christian martyrs must be helped. The American churches know since 50 years about the martyrs in the Communist world. How much have you in your budget for their families?

You answered to my demands above, that your Church has no funds. In Minneapolis a woman who earns 300 dollars a month, with a sick husband and 2 children, gave me 500 dollars, everything she had, for this work. You had no money for it. Then I proposed to you to renounce a substantial part of the salaries. Jesus has taught poverty. It is not with me but with Jesus that you disagree in this point. The Church has money for choir-robes and for Hallowe'ens and has none for families of Christian martyrs who starve? It is ugly that you appeal to love of money which you presume exists in the heart of your pastors to incite them against me in this question. Just 2 days ago, a simple pastor gave 1,000 dollars for this work.

Show me one official bishop of the East who has protested openly against the killing of Christians and poisoning of children with atheism. They would have gone to prison? Why not? Is it wrong to go to prison and to say the truth? Then away with all the prophets of old, with St. John the Baptist, Jesus and all the saints after him, with Jan Huss, Latimer, Zwingli and the millions of others. I venerate these. I think that these were right. I admire St. Ambrose who openly opposed the emperor. So did also St. John Chrysostom. Never has the church venerated a saint stooge. The first canonization of such a one will have to be made by you.

In innumerable nations with 1 billion population, Christians are imprisoned, killed and tortured and children are poisoned with atheism. You boast with a few thousand hymnbooks which have been printed. And these hymnbooks make you to comply with the mass-murderers, to be silent at their crimes, to bring the wolves into the flock. The price is much too high.

If you would have asked the Communist Party of Rumania which is its major desire regarding me, she would have answered: "Stop him from preaching!" In this question, as in many others, the leaders of the World Council of Churches do just what the Communists desire. Wurmbrand should not tell the horrors of Communism.

You stopped me. You did not reprove your colleague of the World Council of Churches who declared publicly that Communism has made no martyrs more since 1920.

Your step is not only harmonized, but also synchronized with those of the Communists. You wrote your circular letter just at the same time when the delegation of the Rumanian tyrants at what is called the Organization of the United Nations (for one-third of the world, not the nations, but their oppressors are represented) complained at the Secretariate that I am allowed to speak in the States. How is it that there is always such a harmony beween the Atheistic Communist mass-murderers and the actions the World Council of Churches?

You assert that the Eastern German bishops are not stooges of the Communists. I can prove that they are. The Communists have stolen countries, they have stolen the school-buildings in our country and in Eastern Germany, too. They have robbed everybody of everything. How would you feel if somebody would steal your church, your car, your house, your furniture? From me and thousands of others, Communists have stolen everything. My former Lutheran Church in Bucharest is now a cinema. In Eastern Germany innumerable pastors passed through prison. The bandit Ulbricht can keep citizens under his leadership only by shooting continually people who try to pass to the West, notwithstanding the Berlin Wall. And now, listen what the Eastern German bishops whom you defend declare about this government of mass-murderers and robbers. I quote their declaration from "Christianity Today" 6. XI 64: "A Christian is in duty bound to respect and accept the political and social structure of the Communist state ... By faith we must also accept the economic structure of this state; the seventh commandment cannot be used as a club against expropriation and collectivization."

If these bishops are right then Elijah who opposed Ahab for the stealing of one vineyard and murder of one Nahab was wrong.

My feelings towards you remain the same of warm love. The peace of God surpasses not only understanding, but also every misunderstanding. Christians can be on opposed positions and love each other notwithstanding.

May God bless you and give you love for his Word for those who endure tortures for this holy Word.

As for me, it is clear that I had to refuse your proposal to work under the supervision of someone associated with the Communist spies of the World Council of Churches. It would have meant to endanger our workers behind the Iron Curtain.

I have proved by documents that your assertions were wrong. In honesty, you are obliged to cancel your former circular letter and to urge all churches to invite the man about whom you write that he has borne the cross 14 years in Communist prisons for the Gospel's sake.

Communists have made us bleeding wounds and you have put salt on the wounds as Jesus saith: "Every sacrifice must be salted with salt."

If you don't retract, I hope that the other president, the faithful pastors and the rank and file Christians will not listen to your recommendation, but protest against it and fight together with the Underground Church against Communism; inviting me to tell them in sermons the truth about these matters.

Yours in Christ Jesus,
Richard Wurmbrand

To the same leader of the World Council of Churches:

Dear Brother:

I received your letter of the 3rd instant.

Your assertion that my reasoning is confused and my thinking blurred is not new to me.

As in other things, leaders of the World Council of Churches are in harmony with the Communist mass-killers and mass-torturers and mass-deceivers in this question too. When, after my first release from prison, thousands flocked to listen to my sermons, the Communists spread all over Rumania the news that I am mad. They used for this purpose their tools in the churches.

My mind may be confused. It would be no wonder after all the things through which I passed. But how is the mind of your pastors? I have a pile of letters from them. What pastors are they if they cannot distinguish between a prophet and a madman? All those who heard me preaching, write that I am a "prophetic voice," "a prophet," "a new St. John," "St. Paul," "St. Basil." You insult your pastors saying that mine is a confused reasoning and a blurred thinking. It means that they do not know how to distinguish the spirits. Not to have this gift disqualifies a man as a pastor.

As for myself, I believe that I am neither a St. Paul, nor have a confused mind. Even if I would know that I have a confused mind, I would not mind it, because I walk on a way on which even the fool cannot err, (Isaiah 35), the way of undeniable faith. I am an ordinary man with ordinary abilities, who has a message from God which cannot be contradicted. For not accepting this my message you will answer before God and until then before your flock.

Christ has taught to teach all the nations, not only those until the Iron Curtain. Have you started a mission to the millions of souls who get lost in Red China, the Soviet Union and the other Communist countries? If not, why? Will you be able to tell God that you had no funds? The cobbler Carey had money to begin a missionary work in India and Hudson Taylor had for China and you had not? My salary when I left Rumania was $28.00 a month. With so much, we made missionary work in a Communist country. So much is sufficient to sustain a worker in a Communist country. Even if I would be a madman, in this question I am absolutely right and you absolutely wrong not to accept immediately my message.

I told you six months ago that families of Christian martyrs must be helped. I have given you their addresses. Did you do it? If not, why? Will you say to God that you had no money when $20.00 a month would have helped a family not to starve? I may be confused, but I speak with authority from God that they must be helped. You may have a straight mind. The greater will be your responsibility not to have accepted my message immediately.

I told you that the Hromadkas and Justinians and Nikolais from the World Council of Churches are traitors and have given you the proof of it. You had either to drive them out immediately from this Christian body or to leave this body. Just today I received a letter that two ministers after having seen my film left forever the World Council of Churches, as members of the Communist Party of Norway left it after having seen my television program. Again a parallelism. World Council of Churches and Communism work together on many points. Those who awake leave both these organizations.

In these three points, who does not accept my words puts himself in conflict with God. This is important, not the considerations about my mind.

Do I love the Communists? The deeds show it. I work all day a very risky work to bring them to Christ. And when you sleep, I pass sleepless nights, praying and weeping for their lost souls. You do not believe that I love them really. Alright! But you must love them. When do you start a mission to the Communists? When Hudson Taylor loved the Chinese, he proved it by such a deed. I did like Hudson Taylor and Carey. What are you doing about this?

It is not true that I reject all the leaders of the official churches in the Communist countries. On the contrary, I greatly admire the Cardinal Wyszinsky, who has been in prison and risks it again opposing Communism. I admire him, although he belongs to an official church. And I pray that the Protestant bishops may take example from him.

How could I appreciate Bishop Miroslave of Prague, who declared on the 12th August, 1958 in Chicago, "there is more religious liberty under the Communists than before"? Has he not heard of the Cardinal Beran and hundreds of Protestants who have been put in jail and tortured? I cannot appreciate Bishop Janos Peter of Hungary, another of the gang of red bishops who lured his brother back from Cairo to Hungary. The brother was there killed.

But I do not reject all the leaders of official churches.

You complain about the bitter spirit of my articles and speeches. Just today I receive a letter from one of your pastors who heard me preaching last Sunday. He says that "Wurmbrand just radiated the love of Christ . . . he shows nothing than Christian love and tender compassion toward those who have persecuted him, those who have been and are his enemies and those who do not believe him." When he preached "we were, in essence, in the very presence of Christ himself." I have a pile of similar letters.

What a bad opinion you have about your pastors when you say that I have a bitter spirit!

There is something else. Not my spirit is bitter, but bitter is the fate of thousands of Christians who are tortured and killed in the Communist camp. Bitter is the fate of their families. Daughters of Christian martyrs are sometimes harlots to be able to support their starving families. Christian priests have been buried alive in China a fortnight ago. I would have expected a Christian bishop to feel and to share this their bitterness and to convene immediately the Church Council to see how they can be helped, instead of complaining that Wurmbrand speaks bitter words, seeing that all his efforts to stir up the leaders of the World Council of Churches to help Christian martyrs and the suffering church are vain. Supposing that everything which you say about me is true, why don't you organize at once a preaching schedule for other pastors of the Underground Church who have not my defects? Let them speak about the martyrs for Christ, they who have suffered. Metropolite Nikolai, the rogue, has been invited. Why not these? It is not me whom you wish to muzzle but the whole suffering church, which has given heroes of faith like these. Not I, everyone who has experienced the horror of Communism must be silenced. This is the order of Moscow, which is obeyed at Geneva.

My message is surely from God. If you accept it, it has sense to correspond further about practical means to fulfill it. If you do not accept it, as I surely will not change, the best is to remain silently in love toward one another. You who have not borne a cross preach about a cross; those who have borne a cross are forbidden to say what they know about it. At the judgement of God you will show me that I have been wrong to put the problem of the relief of families of Christian martyrs and the problem of missionary work behind the Iron Curtain.

How do you hope to succeed in stopping me from preaching when Communists did not succeed? I preached even when I was in solitary confinement, by tapping the Gospel in Morse Code through the wall.

You have an excuse that the council of Catholic bishops has been just like yours. Nearly all the Catholic bishops of Rumania died in prison under tortures. Catholic priests are buried alive in China. American Catholic bishops discuss if it is lawful to eat meat on Friday.

You will say "another bitter attack." It comes from the bitterness of sufferings of Catholics in the Communist camp. My wife was in prison with the Catholic nuns. She described them as angels. Angels are in the hands of brutes. Who can understand the bitterness of such a fate? Think about this bitterness, not about that of my words!

As you have a family, I wish your family all the best. I think with love about your family because most of my family has been killed by dictators supported and highly praised by the Protestant bishops of our country. The one who murdered most of my family was later converted in my house. Is this bitterness . . . or love?

Yours very sincerely,
R. Wurmbrand

To a leader of the Baptist Union of Great Britain
Dear Brother,

Baptists from Great Britain sent me the letter which you addressed to several of them in connection with the persecution of brethren in the Soviet Union.

During a preaching-schedule in Great Britain last month I had informed them about what is happening there. The Baptist Union had neglected its duty to do so. She has not beaten the alarm. She has not mobilized prayer-forces in favor of the persecuted ones. She has not organized the relief for families of Christian martyrs, as if the Russian and the British Christians would not be one body. I had to come from Scandinavia to do this.

When I was beaten at the bottom of the feet, my tongue cried. Now, why did the tongue cry? It was not beaten. But the tongue and the bottom of the feet were one body. If you would feel the pains of the oppressed brethrens as yours, you would have cried since long.

How could you be so badly duped and dupe others? You say that "you have maintained as close contact as possible with the leaders of our churches there." "They tell us that we can really do no good by public protests".

Are you the only one not to know who these leaders are? They are the men of the Communist Secret Police. They have made the denunciations against the brethren who are in prison. They bear the guilt of the imprisonments, tortures and deaths. What good is their advice not to protest?

I know from my own experience how somebody becomes leader of an official church in the Communist camp. Minister deputy for Internal Affairs, General Negrea, proposed me in prison to be released and to become Lutheran bishop. He told me also what would be my duty as a Red bishop: to see that such laws as the ones forbidding Sunday schools for children, youth meetings, religious propaganda should be enforced, to assure the political loyalty towards the Communist tyrants of the church-membership, to denounce the counter-revolutionary elements. If I would have accepted this proposal, I would have been your friend in the World Council of Churches. One of the tasks assigned to me would have been to dupe Western Church leaders about the religious liberty in Rumania and to make them to accept the Communist point of view in political matters, as the World Council of Churches usually does.

In Rumania, the Baptist leadership has been imposed by the Secret Police. I attended the Baptist Congress. When the list proposed by the Communists was proposed, the whole congress shouted, "No". They received only nine votes. Then the representative of the Communist gangsters arose and said: "These have to be the leaders." The attendants at the Congress understood and voted for them as our whole country votes at political "elections" for the bandits who oppress them. This is how the official church leaders in Communist lands are elected, I have seen it with my eyes.

The same is true in Russia. The Baptists who are in prison there, have been jailed because they rebelled against their treacherous leaders and, defying them, organized Sunday schools for children and secret baptisms. I have a pile of excerpts from the Soviet-press, which proves this.

You must not listen to these traitors but organize immediate public protests. The Jews are a wise people. Why do they protest continually against the anti-Semitism there? They know that only by this can they keep Jewry alive in Russia. If you continue to listen to the traitors, the British Baptists will no more listen to you and organize public protests above your head. I have seen in Great Britain many churches lost by the Baptist Union because of its collaboration with the Red church-leaders in the World Council of Churches. I never met a church attracted in the Union because of this. Any businessman would know to draw the right conclusion.

The manner in which you write is shameful. I quote: "There have been incidents in the Soviet Union in which Baptists, . . . have landed themselves on the wrong side of the law". I am used to another style, that of the Bible. St. Paul would have written: "There are in Russia brethren of whom the earth is not worthy, who, with boldness from God, dared to continue the holy work although they knew that they will give their lives for this. These are saints and martyrs who will have part of the first resurrection, from which all those who compromise with Communism will be excluded."

If the first Christians would have obeyed the laws of Nero, if Luther would have obeyed the laws of the Pope, you would not have been today a leader of the Baptist Union.

Every phrase of yours tends to cover the crimes of the Communists, as other leaders of the World Council of Churches do, too. You write that in Russia "it is not a crime to possess a Bible," instead of saying that it is a crime of the Communist to make that the people should have no Bibles.

You write "I was assured that if and when our Baptist brethren pressed for a new printing of the Scriptures, this would be sympathetically considered." Now, why do the Baptist leaders of Russia not press for this if the publishing of Bibles is only a question of pressure from their side? Because they are men of the Communists. Can you imagine a real Baptist not desiring that the Bible should be printed?

You mislead the British Baptists writing "I am sure our Baptist brethren in Russia itself will take steps to care for the wives and families of any who are involved in difficulties with authorities" (what a nice expression for martyrs tortured to death!) Baptists pass through prisons in Russia since 50 years. Did you ask the Baptist leadership in Russia if they have ever given one penny for their families? Don't you know that the churches are not allowed to have any charitable activity in Communist countries? Two Christian ladies who helped my son, while my wife and I were in prison, were so beaten for this that they are cripples since 14 years. The lady who took my son in her house, was sentenced to eight years of prison for helping families of "counter-revolutionaries." Who does not know such things, should not be a leader.

The relief for families of Christian martyrs can be organized only in the West. As a matter of fact, we started already this organization in Baptist churches in Great Britain, taking great care that you, who collaborate with the tools of Communists, should never know any detail. Many Baptist churches in Great Britain, where I preached, are ready rather to quit you and the World Council of Churches than the martyrs. First help to families of Christian martyrs went already and we just got the news that the well organized trip has been successful. To such an action you should give your support, if you are a child of God.

Yours sincerely,
R. Wurmbrand

Open Letter to a German leader of the World Council of Churches

I am a man who has come out recently after 14 years of Communist prison and from behind the Iron Curtain.

As for many years I was in solitary confinement and, except the last months of prison life, have never seen a newspaper, I did not know how you have changed.

I remained with what I had known about you from times before. I had read the collection of your sermons in which you criticized the Hitler-Regime on futile, secondary matters, not saying one word against what was really important: the terror, the cruelties, racism, totalitarianism, the spirit of revenge and militarism, the tendency to conquer the world, the anti-Christianity. But the little you said was enough to irritate a dictatorship, which tolerated not the slightest opposition. You were put in prison. Suffering sanctifies. When you came out of prison, your sermons were on a much higher level. Now you spoke about the national sin of Germans. It was not an easy task. I admired you for having had the courage to do so.

Afterwards I was put in prison. I did not hear anymore about you. When I came out of prison, people told me that you are now on the side of the Communists. I know that there exists much slander in the world. Jesus has been called a devil. I payed no attention to what I heard against you.

Now it happened that we both arrived at the same time in Norway and I read your declarations in the newspapers.

Dear brother, you simply say consciously things which are untrue.

Let us take one assertion after the other:

1) "Divine services are not forbidden in Eastern Germany under the Communists." That is all what you have to say. It is like as if asked about one's honesty, I would answer that he has a beautiful moustache. You wished to give the impression of religious liberty in Eastern Germany.

Do you know that just last week Eastern Germany has forbidden the World Congress of the Lutheran World Federation, which should have been held in Weimar? Why did you not mention this?

Divine services are not forbidden. Neither are they forbidden in Rumania. In Eastern Germany, Rumania and in many Communist countries, except Russia, thousands of churches are open, liturgies are accomplished and sermons are delivered. This dupes the Westerner.

But you should have known and told the trick. In these countries, priests and pastors and rabbies are free to say that God is good. They are not allowed to say that the devil is bad.

What do I mean by this?

St. John the Baptist would never have been beheaded because he said: "Repent, the Kingdom of Heaven is near." He was beheaded when he said: "You, Herod, are bad." Jesus has not been crucified for the Sermon on the Mount, but because he said: "Woe unto you, hypocrite pharisees! You are a generation of vipers."

So, to a certain extent, if you don't do it with too much ability from God and don't attract great masses of people around you, you are free to preach in Eastern Germany and many satellite countries that God is good. But nowhere is the pastor allowed to say that the cruelties, atrocities and atheism of Communism are from the devil. And every service in which the devil is not denounced is not really divine service.

Recently we heard from Tito that his minister of internal affairs, Rancovici, had put microphones in Tito's office. Czechoslovakian diplomats were accused of having tried to put microphones in the Department of State of the United

States of America. Imagine now if in every church there are ears of the Communist Secret Police! Is the pastor free to say what God puts on his heart?

Jesus saith: "The truth sets free." But the contrary is also a fact. Only freedom gives truth. Where the pastor is muzzled, where he has to fear of years of prison for a word of criticism in his sermon, there can be no truth. In the Communist countries, the truth hides itself in the Underground Church, the martyr-church, the most real one. It is the honour of Eastern Germany that it has given martyrs.

2)   You assert that "the conflict between East and West appertains to the past. The actual conflict is that between rich and poor nations." Then you speak about the exploitation and oppression of Negroes.

Are the Eastern countries avowed dictatorships of a militant atheist Party? Do they all propagate the Leninist doctrine that every religion must be uprooted? Is private property of means of production forbidden? Is it true that farms have been collectivized? That in a country like Rumania you cannot have even a barbershop of your own?

Is it true that the Western countries — except a few like Spain, Portugal, etc., — are democratic and that every religion is free? In Western Germany even such a queer religion as yours, which praises the tortures and mass-killer of Christians is free. You say that since 1920 there have been no more martyrs in the Communist camp. How free you are! A Russian would not be allowed to say so. He is obliged to say that Stalin has been a mass-murderer. And Stalin murdered until 1953. And after him, the anti-Christian terror continued.

Have you really not heard about the trial of Cardinal Mindszenty? What about your brother, the Lutheran bishop Ordass of Hungary? Were these arrested before 1920? Have you heard that nearly all the Catholic bishops of Rumania died in prison? Do you know that the Greek-Catholic church of Rumania has been liquidated in 1950 and that hundreds were arrested and tortured then? Do you know that Orthodox personalities have been arrested in Rumania a month ago? That in Hungary Catholic priests have been put in prison for having asked children if they believe in God?

Is it true that in the West there exist religious and political liberties and the liberty to have private property?

How can you answer then that the conflict has dissappeared? If you believe that Christianity is the truth and the Communists wish to uproot the truth, how can ever the conflict between light and darkness disappear?

You put instead of the conflict between East and West the conflict between rich and poor nations. But is it not Communism which brings with it every-where poverty? You are a German. Why don't you compare the standard of living in Western and Eastern Germany? Then you would see who are the greater exploiters: the Capitalists or the Communists.

You are against any unjust made to a colored man. So am I. But why do you not mention the anti-Semitism in Russia and all other Communist coun-tries? Do you know that in Kiev, a town with 350,000 Jews, there exists only one synagogue with no rabbi? The same situation in Vilnius, Lithuania. But Russia is taboo. We must speak against racial discrimination everywhere, except in Russia. They are free to do what they like. Those like you and your colleagues from the World Council of Churches will not protest.

You declare yourself against the war in Vietnam. You liked it when the Americans freed Germany from Nazism which killed 6 million Christians and Jews. You should rejoice that America is fighting as in times before against a cruel dictatorship. But this time you don't agree.

Your role is not to take the defense of the oppressed. It is another one: to be always on the side of the Russians, who have stolen half of your fatherland and to be against the free world.

You say that in Eastern Germany 90% of the youth goes to "Jugendweihe" the Communist ceremony, because confirmation in church is a dead habit. I can believe that the imposition of hands by a man like you can be a dead habit. When a faithful pastor or bishop does it, Christ blesses. But you speak? Don't you remember the 99% who voted with Hitler in all plebiscites? Did you not explain this in times before by the terror? In all Communist countries, at all elections, 99% vote for the Government. With whom else should they vote? With us a joke is made that, when God created Adam, he created only one woman, Eve. Then he said to Adam: "You can choose any woman you like as your wife." But only Eve was there. So it is with all Communist ceremonies. You have to accept them or to bear all kinds of disadvantages in schools and employments. You know it and say consciously the untruth.

How can you assert that Seigerwasser, the entrusted of the East-German Communist Government is a Communist but not unfriendly to the Church? To be a Communist means to be a Leninist. And Lenin has declared openly that the uprooting of religion is his program.

I am sorry about you.

When I came out of prison, a woman told me: "Now you have suffered much. Be careful not to sin any more, otherwise the value of your suffering will be cancelled."

You may not have had such a good adviser. And after having suffered much, you became an apologist for Communist politics.

Open Answer to a Confidential Letter written by an important religious personality to all the Norwegian Lutheran bishops

The Underground Church, the martyr church from behind the Iron Curtain, abandoned and sometimes betrayed by many religious leaders of the West, has taken its measures and self-defense.

It has its own men in all great religious bodies of the West: in the World Council of Churches, in the Lutheran World Federation, in the Federation of Reformed Churches, in Baptist Unions, in Bible Societies, in Missionary Councils. Sometimes these men are bishops, sometimes typists, sometimes those who sweep the floor. But all have a keen eye for everything which is of interest for the one billion people oppressed by the Communists and inform us. We are better informed about what happens in the Western religious world than many Western religious leaders.

So it happened that a confidential letter sent by the Norwegian Bible Society to the Norwegian bishops has arrived in our hands, even before it arrived in the hands of those to whom it was written. The Eastern Church is not abandoned by everybody. It has friends.

In this confidential letter, you disassociate yourself from my secret Evangelistic and Bible-spreading activity, giving as motive that this has had as result the increasing of anti-Christian persecution in the Communist countries and has closed doors for Christian activity, which otherwise would have opened.

The author of this letter has spoken with me only a few days ago. He promised to grant a request which I made. He gave not the slightest sign that he has anything to reprove in my activity. At this time, he had written behind my back a letter against me. Jesus teaches otherwise in Matthew 16.

But now to the facts: When I spoke in the West about the torturing and killing of Christians behind the Iron Curtain, when I spoke about the closing of churches and the forbidding of the word of God, my assertions were contested. I was told that these things belong to the past and that now there is a liberalization. When I replied: "If you suppose that there is a liberalization, let us profit of it and try to pump into the Communist countries as many Bibles as possible", I was answered that this would lead to new terrorist persecutions. When I asked again: "What liberalization is this in which you have to fear of bringing into a country Bibles," I was left without further answer.

The connection which you make between the increased anti-Christian terror in Communist countries and my public demasking of it and asserting that, despite of it, we will make missionary work behind the Iron Curtain is founded on nothing.

The whole Islamic press complains against a new wave of anti-Islamic terror in Soviet-Russia. The Dalai Lama declared that the Chinese Communists are simply outrooting Buddhism in Tibet. The same happens in Russia. Authorized Jewish leaders complain about a new wave of anti-Semitism. Against this wave protested even Bertrand Russell and Jean Paul Sartre, who are otherwise entirely on the side of the Communists.

For persecuting of Christians, you have found the guilty: it is Wurmbrand who has made public declarations against the Communists. But who is the guilty for anti-Semitism, for new anti-Moslem and anti-Buddhist measures? How is it that a religious leading personality of Norway does not understand that the anti-Christian attitude of the Communist rulers is a result of the teachings of Marx and Lenin and not of a simple man, who demasked it and declared his decision to oppose it?

But supposing that I am a very strong personality and that a few articles and sermons of mine have been the cause of anti-religious measures as far as Tibet and Turkestan, how is it that in the Communist camp, there is a new wave of terror against socialists? You must have heard about the case of Mihailov of Yugoslavia. Am I guilty also of this? Supposing that this guilt can also be put upon me, how is it that there is a new wave of Communists killing Communists? Have you not heard about the new purge (purge means mass-killing of Communists) in China? Who is guilty here?

Communism is a religion of hatred. Khruschev hated his comrade Stalin so much that he took his corpse out of his grave. Then Breshnev hated him and threw him away as a dirty rag. Others are preparing the same fate for Breshnev. Of the cruelties of Communism, the guilty are the Communists or the devil who is behind them. It is false to blame for it those who oppose Communism.

When the Bible Society has been forbidden in Russia, I was a little child. It has been forbidden in nearly all the satellite countries when I was in prison. Who was guilty then?

If there is somebody guilty in the Christian camp, these are leaders of religious bodies who compromise with Communism.

When the Russians occupied our countries, the Bible Society did not fulfill its duty to provide us instantly with Russian Gospels. I had to print them secretly, without its knowledge. If we would have awaited the Bible Society to do it, they would not have appeared, so slow is it in its reaction. It does a very valuable work in many countries, but she is inadequate for the specific needs of the Communist countries, where things must be done secretly and quickly.

The museum of the British Bible Society boasts with Bibles printed and smuggled secretly centuries ago. When, inspired by what they have seen in this museum, British Christians tried to smuggle Bibles into Russia and were caught, the British Bible Society, instead of disassociating itself from the Soviet authorities which forbid the Word of God, instead of disassociating itself from the Russian newspaper "Trud" which declared the Bible to be "poison," disassociated itself publicly from these four Christians, saying that it has nothing to do with them.

How did the first Christians spread the Word of God? Did they cease spreading it because a Nero forbade it? How did the Reformers spread it? Did they ask the Inquisition? Should we not have the same faith as that of our fathers?

When the Bible Societies had their so called world congress in America this spring, 1/3 of the world was not represented. The representatives of the Underground Church from behind the Iron and Bamboo Curtains were not called to tell of the hunger after the Word of God in these countries and to give practical advice what could be done. You can feast very well without them.

Therefore the "European Christian Missions" in Britain, "Mission to Europe's Millions in the USA", and other missions have taken the providing of Communist countries with the Word of God in their own hands, giving also regular audits about all the sums connected for this purpose.

We will continue also to oppose publicly the anti-Christian terror and the treachery of all religious leaders who compromise with Communism.

Can this cause victims? Yes. When Moses began his work of freeing the Jewish slaves, the first result was that the state of these slaves became worse.

The norm they had to fulfill in brick-makings had been increased. The fact that the apostles spread the Gospel had as one of its results that thousands were thrown before the lions. How much blood has the Reformation cost? Was it a mistake? The fight of Norwegian patriots against the Nazis had also as result reprisals. Were the Norwegian patriots wrong to fight? But in the end, Communism will be conquered by Christ. Those who suffer in Communist prisons, the leaders of the underground churches, with whom we are connected, they who would have most to fear, send us secret messages asking us to continue. And we will listen to the voice of the martyr church, not to the voice of the cowards of the West.

You had a good motive to write a letter to the bishops. You should have protested that a leader of the church was allowed to spread in Norway his lie that since 1920 Communists have made no martyrs. You should have informed the Bishops of the thousands who have been killed since then for spreading the Bible.

Your letter is beside the point!

Another task lays before the Norwegian bishops. Norway develops a great missionary activity, but it stops at the Iron Curtain. Now, all missionary societies are valuable, but if we don't win for Christ the Communists, the most aggressive foes of Christianity, they will fulfill in this generation their program. They will invade Norway as well as the other Western countries and finished it will be with all your Missions. Mission to the Communists, with all risks, even with risk of adorning new heads with the martyr-crown, is a question of life or death.

But I must assure you that the underground workers of our organization are not only brave. They are wise too. Of the workers whom we have behind the Iron Curtain, no one has ever been arrested, as the helpers of Communism in the World Council and similar bodies have never discovered our men in these institutions.

The first Christians led their missionary work secretly and we must quietly do missionary work in Communist countries because it will have to be secret.

Many can sleep quietly while one billion of men are kept under a terror which forbids the Word of God, the source of salvation. But there are others who have Christ's passion for souls, who know what it is to hunger after the living water. I have been without a Bible for 14 years and I desired it more than I desired my wife and my child.

Yours sincerely,
R. Wurmbrand

P.S. May I just add that Jewish, Moslem and Buddhist organizations provide secretly their fellow-believers in the Communist countries with their holy Scriptures and objects of cult. So do the Catholics too. Should only Protestants not do it?

To a leader of the British Council of Churches,

Dear Brother,

When we met, you told me that you had to sit at my feet and to learn from me. I have expected since then that you would write to me, asking from me lessons, not because I consider myself very wise and cultured, but for another motive. As in the first Church of the Bishop of Rome was considered the senior Bishop, because Rome gave the greatest number of martyrs, so the Underground Church from behind the Iron Curtain, whose member I am, should be the senior in the Universal Church today, it giving in this century the greatest number of men tortured and killed for Christ.

But since we saw each other, it seems that instead of taking lessons from the Underground Church, you took lessons from the Communists and so you arrived to write the article published in a British newspaper, only what you learned about Marxism was wrong.

It is not so that Stalin's Russia was far removed from the vision of Marx. It was the very fulfilling of his vision. Marx writes in "The Capital", "Violence is the midwife which takes the Socialist society out of the womb of the Capitalist one." Marx criticizes the Commune of Paris for not having killed enough counter-revolutionaries. Marx, although himself a Jew, was an anti-Semite and classified the Jews as parasites in his book "The Jewish Problem". Marx says "It is only the evil side which makes history" and he conscientiously always appealed to the evil side. Stalin, in his terror, in his anti-Christianity and anti-Semitism, was a faithful disciple of Karl Marx.

That Stalin fought against Christianity is easy to understand, but why should you, a Pastor, belittle it? You write that in the 19th century, "Christianity utterly failed to offer men what they needed", and that it was "wedded to the social machinery of injustice." Have you really never heard about Wilberforce? Don't you know that it is due to this Christian that slave trade was abolished in the 19th century? Did you never hear about Abraham Lincoln, the Christian who abolished slavery in the States in the 19th century? Did you never hear about the Christian, Lord Shaftesbury, who introduced the 8-hour working day and abolished children's work? If you, who comply with Marxism, would only read Marx attentively and would see how he, in his book "The Capital", expresses his admiration for the Christian factory inspectors who started the campaign which changed radically the situation of the working class in Great Britain and afterwards in the world!

Could you please tell me the names of the social assassins who had the best pews in the Church at that time, as you write? You will find in the 19th century not one Bishop or leading personality of the Church who deserves such appreciation.

I cannot tell you how scandalized I am that a Pastor writes that Karl Marx, "quite rightly dismissed religion". First of all, you speak again as a man who has not studied Marx. You know Marx as little as the Christian religion. Marx has never dismissed religion. Marx was a double hearted man. He writes in the prologue of "The Capital" that Christianity, especially in its Protestant form, is the ideal religion for the re-making of lives destroyed by sin. He writes that "religion is the soul of a soulless society", that it is "the spirit of the spiritless society", that it is "a cry of suffering hearts". It is a dishonor to a Protestant Pastor to dismiss a religion to which he has sworn allegiance. Marx did not do this.

Notwithstanding many beautiful words which Marx and Engels spoke about religion, you are wrong in saying that the "old faith" (Christianity) and Marxism are alike. Your duty should have been different. Love and seduction use the same vocabulary. A young man who desires a girl honestly for marriage and one who wishes to lead her astray for one night use the same words: "I love you". The role of a Christian Pastor is to discern the intentions behind the words, to demask the wolf behind the sheep's skin. Marxism proceeds from a double hearted man, from an anti-Semite Jew, from a man who highly appreciated Christianity and hated it at the same time. Therefore, wherever it has come to power, it has meant mass murder, torture, poisoning of youth with atheism, destruction of all the high values of life. The Christians did very right to declare an ideological war on Marxism. By this they did not disregard the Master's command to love enemies as you say. The Master Himself, in His time, led ideological wars, but sacrificed Himself for the good of those against whom He led the ideological war. Exactly the same, the Underground Church behind the Iron Curtain leads an ideological war against Communism and sacrifices itself at the same time to win the Communists for Christ.

I wonder also that you complain about the many tracts of land and about the shares which the church has. What would your salary be without the property of the Church of England? If you are against having property, why do you not pass at once to fulfilling the Master's command and being as poor as a Pastor of the Underground Church? In that Church your desire is fulfilled. My salary, when I left Rumania, was £8 a month. We, four persons, could live on this salary. Do the same! But it is immoral to be a profiteer of the shares and lands kept by a Church and to defame her because she has them.

It is also not true that the liquidation of Communists by Hitler has happened without a murmur of Christian protest. From what world do you come that you have never heard about Boendorffer, Faulhaber and the others who dared to protest against Hitlerism under Hitler's dominion?

You mislead the British people by saying that the great confrontation between Communism and Christianity has ended. You say that just when Red Guards in China have closed the last Christian churches and are cutting off ears, tongues, legs of Christian prisoners in pails. You say it just when Baptist preachers in Russia have been sentenced for the crime of having told children about Christianity. You say it just when "Isvestia" accuses Baptists of teaching ritual murder, just as the Jews were accused in times before. Has the fight of the Godless against Christianity ceased in Russia?

In your appreciation of Togliatti's Testament you show again your lack of knowledge about Communism. Fifty years before Togliatti, Lenin wrote, "We do not only admit into the Social-Democratic Party all those who still retain faith in God, but must redouble our efforts to recruit them. We are absolutely opposed to the slightest affront to these workers' religious convictions. We recruit them in order to educate them and not in order to carry on an active struggle against religion." On the same occasion, Lenin said that even a Priest could become a Party member. Communists have always had an elastic and opportunistic attitude towards believers. The main aim for them is the conquest of power. If they can conquer it by abandoning the fight against atheism, they will do it. In my fatherland, the Communists crossed themselves and kissed holy images as every orthodox until they had the power to uproot religion. Then they showed their true face. The reader has the right to expect from a Pastor who writes about Communism to know these things and not to be deceived by the opportunistic words of Togliatti.

You say that only in Russia the Communist party and the Church "hang on grimly. Elsewhere the floodgates are wide open." — Only in Russia? What about China where the last Churches have been closed and the statues of Mao Tse-Tung put on altars? What about Poland where Cardinal Wyszinsky is treated as an international burglar and not allowed to leave the country and Billy Graham is not allowed to enter it? What about Rumania where Christians are in prison for the crime of having taught Christianity to children? What about Cuba with its persecution of the Catholic Church?

That active membership of the Church is no bar to party membership is also not something new. I have already quoted Lenin. I could quote also Yaroslavsky who tells the story of an old party member who even after the Revolution wrote on the top of a party questionnaire, "In the Name of the Father and of the Son and of the Holy Spirit, Amen." Even as late as in 1921 the Central Committee of the Russian Communist Party issued instructions that tolerance should be shown towards believing party members. The aim has always been the same; to get the support of Christians for the atheistic aims of Communism.

A Pastor should know how to distinguish the real sheep from the wolves in sheep's skin and should not make pacts with the mass murderers and torturers of Christians.

Of all the names which you quote, I would pick out Hromadka of Prague, and arch-traitor of Christianity.

The Communists have published that Stalin killed millions of innocent people. Mikoyan was his right hand in doing this and I have seen the picture and read the speech of Hromadka when he visited Mikoyan. He did not ask him to repent of his crimes. He smiled at him and praised him. Neither Hromadka nor any other like him ever had a word of praise for Christians who were martyred by the Communists.

When I was still in prison, the Rumanian Secret Police made me the proposal to become a Lutheran Bishop and to represent the Church in Geneva. The condition was to use Geneva for the purposes of Communism. I refused the proposal. I know what the Bishops from the East who came to Geneva are worth and who has made them Bishops. It was not the Church. It was the Secret Police. The World Council of Churches believes in speaking with the

Church of the East — and speaks with the Secret Police.

In the camp of real Christians the days of dogmatism will never be over. The Christian dogmas are the truth, and in the Communist camp thousands die yearly for this truth. Well living Pastors of the West, profiteers of land and shares kept by the Church which they attack, may abandon dogmas which they know as little as they know Communism. We will remain with the faith of our fathers.

The Church with all its mistakes and failures represents not only God, but also humanity, its deepest needs, peace and freedom. Where the Church disappears, we have the horrors of Hitlerism and Bolshevism.

Surely Christians and Communists have a ground of common action in the Communist camp. Christians give their backs and Communists give the whips with which to whip. We give our liberty and they give us prisons. We give our lives and they give the bullets to take them away. We give Churches, they give the means of destroying them. (In pre-Communist Moscow there were a thousand Orthodox Churches. Now there are only forty.) We give our children and Communists give atheistic poison to them.

Never have the world's hungry been fed by the Communists. Wherever Communism comes, the hungry are hungrier than before. My fatherland was in times past the granary of Europe. Now our peasants have no bread. Russia lives upon the wheat of America.

May I remind you of what Isaiah says, "Woe unto them that call evil good and good evil, that put darkness for light and light for darkness."

In everything you write, you take the responsibility of the future of the British Empire and of the Church. Out of love I write to you, asking you that before you write again about Christianity and Communism you should study both thoroughly. What I have said to you is not just the opinion of a man. I express the feelings and the thoughts of the peoples and of the Churches horribly oppressed by Communism and which were in their right to expect from a Pastor that he should show friendship to them and not to their oppressors.

Yours very sincerely,
R. Wurmbrand

"A BISHOP HAS SPOKEN"

(An article published by me in Norwegian newspapers.)

My interviews and articles have arisen a discussion pro and contra. It is not my intention to answer to everybody.

A "bourgeois priest" said that I cannot be considered as an objective witness, because I have suffered. I understand that this priest has not given his name. But I would have liked to know his religion. Of the Christian religion he cannot be, because this religion considers as the embodied truth the One who has suffered most, the Crucified One. Of Jewish religion he is not, because this considers as revelators of truth the Prophets, who have suffered much. Buddhism considers suffering as source of truth. Hinduists lay on spikes and submit themselves to self-inflicted heavy sufferings in order to arrive to truth. What religion excludes a man from objective truth because he suffered? I know only the Epicurean, the religion of those who consider the enjoyance of pleasures of life as supreme truth.

Somebody else reproaches to me that I am partial, whereas a leader of the World Council of Churches, who has been in Norway at the same time as I and praised Communism, has been neutral. When Norway was oppressed by the Nazis, what has been the right attitude? To be partial or to be neutral? We have always to be on the side of the oppressed. The Bolsheviks oppress one-third of the world. I am not neutral, but on the side of the tyrannized.

Others don't like that I am not a pacifist. Were these men pacifists when Norway was oppressed or did they like it that the American and British army came to deliver them? They are pacifists when another's fatherland is stolen. No, Pacifism is not Christian. St. Francis d'Assissi said: "Don't shoot brother wolf, because he is also a creature of God." If brother wolf does not give guarantee that he will not eat sister sheep, the shepherd has to shoot the wolf, if he has four legs or only two. Jesus taught us to love our enemies, but not only our enemies. We have to love our brethren, too. And if enemies attack the life and liberty of our brethren, if gangsters attack children, if Nazis burn Jews and Bolsheviks kill Christians, it is a Christian duty to fight.

An American leader of the World Council of Churches has made me the honour to criticize my sayings in his interview.

Why he chose just me as the object of his polemic, I don't know. I would have expected that he will speak out against his colleague of the World Council of Churches, who asserted in Norway that since 1920 the Communists have made no martyrs. My honored opponent knows that this is not true. But he did not disassociate himself from this man's lie. I expected that he, as an American, will polemise with the many Norwegians who attack America, because of its war in Vietnam, saying that as it was right for the Americans to free Norway from a yoke, so it is right for them to defend Asia from the Communist yoke, much more terrible than the Nazi one. But no. The only one from whom he found right to disassociate himself was I.

In a subtle manner, he took the defense of the thesis, contested by me, that there is religious liberty in the Communist countries. He said that in them you can preach "more or less" the Gospel. An essential part of the Gospel is fight against sin. The greatest sin happening in this century in mankind is the torturing, imprisoning and killing of millions of people by the Communists, the poisoning of the whole youth with atheism. And not only against the Bible do the Communists fight. I have before me excerpts of the Chinese Communist press: "The ideas of Shakespeare belong to the ideology of the exploiting classes and we cannot allow them to be spread around ... They are basically opposed to Socialist collectivism." Balzac must be forbidden because "he praises the reactionary theory of humanity." Victor Hugo must be forbidden, because "he has the final aim to strengthen bourgeois society". Harm is done to a Communist by listening to Beethoven's Ninth Symphony. "The idea of bourgeois-humanist love praised in the choral part causes illusions. Interest in Western bourgeois classical music can only paralyze the revolutionary will", etc., etc.

You will say: "These are the Chinese Communists. The Russians are not so." Nearly daily, you can read in the "Pravda" that the ideological differences between Russia and China are small and that the Russians call the Chinese to unite with them in the fight against everything which is beautiful in humanity.

There exists no preaching of the Gospel, without fighting against the sin of Communism. Can my opponent tell me one Communist country where you can freely fight against Communism as sin, denouncing it to be from the devil?

Where my opponent does not contest my assertions, I leave him. Should I polemise with what he saith that "sport has done the most to make disappear the racial differences"? He must know better than I. I knew from American history that the one who freed the Negroes from slavery was not a sportmanager, but Abraham Lincoln and that he did it out of Christian motives. I knew that the one who has destroyed slave-trade has been Wilberforce and that he did it out of Christian motives.

Let us come back to the problem of Communism. I asserted that the representatives of the Orthodox Church in Geneva are Soviet agents. Here I got the answer: "I cannot pronounce myself with the same assurance like Wurmbrand." The Church is the pillar of truth and a church leader represents the church. He has to answer with "yes" or "no".

Jesus simply refused to speak with religious leaders who said that they cannot speak with assurance about St. John the Baptist if his work is from God or from men.

But I will help my opponent to arrive at assurance:

In 1950, the Greek-Catholic church of Rumania has been liquidated, all its clergy and members being obliged by force to enter in the Orthodox church, the hierarchy of which had compromised with the Communists. At this occasion, all Greek-Catholic bishops, innumerable priests, monks, nuns and hundreds of peasants have been imprisoned, tortured. The bishops died nearly all in prison. The one who presided this bloody operation has been Patriarch Justinian. He is personally guilty of killing bishops of Catholicism, with whom the American Protestants lead theological discussions. Would it not have been right to take the defense of the tortured Catholic bishops and to not receive with great honour at Geneva the Patriarch Justinian, the killer of Christians?

Does he know that all the monks and nuns under the age of 60 have been obliged to leave monasteries, those who refused being arrested? Does he know that blood flew at this operation, too? Does he know that the decree is signed by the Patriarch Justinian, received with honour by the World Council of Churches?

Does he really consider as he saith the representatives of the Russian church as "men of moral integrity", when Archpriest Borovoi declared at the last session of the World Council of Churches that Russia is an example of friendly collaboration between Christians and Socialist revolutions? Did Borovoi not know about many thousands of priests killed? Did he not know about many millions of Christian laymen killed by the Socialist revolution? If he had no other source of information, he could have read in Khruschev's speech at the 20th Congress of the Communist Party how many millions have been killed. A man who sustains that killers and killed cooperate at the producing of the phenomenon of death, a man who mocks the sufferings of the Russian martyr-church is "a man of moral integrity"? Then, what kind of a man is the man who gives lightly such certificates?

Does my opponent not know that Hromadka, the Czechoslovakian personality at the World Council, praised publicly Mikoyan, the right hand of Stalin in killing millions of Christians? This also is moral integrity?

In your interview there was not a word about the martyrs, not a word about the Underground Church, not a word of sympathy to Cardinal Wyszinsky, hindered to travel, as international burglars are normally hindered.

You also avoided wisely to pronounce yourself about my assertion that neither the World Council of Churches, nor the Lutheran World Federation has ever given one crown for the families of Christian martyrs in Russia or Rumania. How is it that children of Christian martyrs who applied to the World Council for a scholarship to enable them to study theology and go then to fight in the martyr-church did not even get replies, whereas members of the Communist Party sent to study theology, to become the future faked Bolshevik-bishops, get scholarships?

America is more and more awake. I have known families who left churches because of their participation in the treacherous activity of the World Council. You will hardly tell me the name of one family which was won for your church by this activity.

The hearts of the real Christians of your country are on the side of the Underground Church, the martyr-church behind the Iron and Bamboo-curtain. Without your knowledge, your church-members and these of other churches sustain many hundred underground workers there. Without your knowledge, tens of thousands of Gospels are smuggled in. Without your participation, the families of martyrs are helped.

My hope is that my opponent will join henceforth his own flock in sustaining the Underground Church in Communist countries.

THE LIE ABOUT
RELIGIOUS LIBERTY
IN THE COMMUNIST CAMP

With very few honourable exceptions, such as that of the leadership of the Catholic church of Poland, stooges of the Communists are posing as shepherds of Christ's flock.

We will begin immediately with facts proving this.

Below we give excerpts from "The Instructive Letter" of the Committee of the Evangelistic Baptist Christians of the Soviet Union. The letter is dated 1960, and is in Vigour right now:

PARAGRAPH 3. "The elder presbyter must know and remember that the principal charge of a divine service actually is not the attraction of new members."

PAGE 1. PARAGRAPH 4. "One of the duties of an older presbyter is to suppress unhealthy missionary activities."

PAGE 2. PARAGRAPH 2. "The elder presbyter ... must avoid in our congregations the unhealthy practice of running after quantities of members."

PAGE 3. PARAGRAPH 2. "The elder presbyter ... must not care about preaching."

PAGE 3. PARAGRAPH 5. "Less sermons and fulfilling of spiritual works ... strict fulfilling of the Soviet legislation on cults" (legislation which forbids the preaching of the Gospel to all creatures).

PAGE 4. PARAGRAPH 4. "The presbyter should not allow tendencies in divine worship in the sense of urgent attraction of new members." (No altar calls are permitted.)

PAGE 7. PARAGRAPH 3. "We must strive to reduce the baptism of young ones between 18 and 30 years of age to a minimum."

PAGE 9. PARAGRAPH 6. "Children of pre-school and school age should not be allowed to attend, as a rule, religious services." (*Nauka i Religia,* Science and Religion, the Moscow Atheist magazine tells us that on Easterdays Communists are watching around the churches, forbidding parents to bring the children with them.)

The "Instructive Letter" continues: "In the past, not taking in considera-
tion enough the Soviet law on cults...there happened baptisms of men
younger than 18. Charities were given from the funds of the churches. Special assemblies for Bible studies and other purposes were organized. It was
permitted to recite poems. There have been excursions of believing youth.
Illegal relief funds were organized. There have been meetings for instructing
preachers and choir leaders...and there have been other breakings of the
Soviet laws. All this must be uprooted now in our churches."

This letter speaks for itself.

A church could not work, neither fulfill its duties towards Christ in such
conditions.

A parallel, Underground Church, had to be created.

What else would every faithful Protestant pastor or layman of America
do, if such instructions were given to him?

Who really represents the Protestants of Russia? The stooges of the
Communists who have written this letter and who are recognized by the
World Baptist Alliance and the World Council of Churches — or the Under-
ground Church, represented nowhere in international Christian bodies?

But the "letter of instruction" says very little concerning the whole story.

We have before us a letter signed by 116 members of the Baptist Church
in Kiev (Russia). They write: "Since decades, the Evangelic Baptist Christians are without rights, witness of which fact are the systematic repressions,
beatings, arrests, trials, searches, the destruction and confiscation of prayer
houses, the taking away of children, the interdiction of worships, the discrimination against believers in factories and colleges, the stirring up of the
public opinion against the believers by lying and slandering inventions in
the press, etc."

On the 16th of May, 1966, some 500 delegates of churches from 130
towns assembled before the building of the Central Committee of the Communist Party in Moscow to protest against these things.

The brethren of the church in Kiev, which had also sent 14 members to
participate at this demonstration, tell us in their letters what happened: "The
men (if they can be called men) of the KGB, the Russian secret police,
soldiers and regular policemen surrounded the brethren and beat them bru-
tally: they tore out their hair, they beat their heads against the wall and
against the asphalt, they strangled them, they beat them with bottles on their
heads, etc. All this happened in the presence of a multitude of assembled
men." The fate of the majority of the delegation is unknown.

"The repression before the building of the Central Committee gave the mood for simliar actions of the local authorities."

Here is an example:

"On the 23rd of May, the Kiev's congregation of Evangelic Baptist Christians had its usual service in the wood. The congregation gathered for the third year on the same place in the wood, during the spring and summer time, informing about this every year the local and central state organs. The unusualness of the choice of the place of worship is explained by the fact that the private houses of believers cannot seat all visitors, who are 400, and our prayer houses on Lenin Street No. 53 and on Jelianskoi Street 104 were confiscated in the years of the cult personality." (By this the "stalinist" times are meant. Stalin has been denounced by Khrushchev as a robber, but what he robbed has remained well robbed.)

They explain further in their letter that there exists a recognized church in Kiev, but which is lead by the stooges of the Communists, who allow their interference in church matters.

"From the very beginning of the divine service on the 22nd of May, 1966, the believers were surrounded by the police; the men of the Secret Police (the KGB), who came in great number on buses, surpassing the number of believers. Not giving the possibility to make the concluding prayer, on a signal of General-Major Dehtiarev (whom we specially recommend to the prayers of Christians . . . my note!), who led this operation, all of the Secret Police who were mobilized for this purpose threw themselves from the wood on the believers and gave them a beating like that given to the delegates in Moscow. Without any distinction, these sadists, with and without uniform, beat not only men, but also women, children and old people. They tore their hair, threw them upon the earth, beat them with their feet and fists and tried to chase the believers into the depth of the forest, far away from the railway station which was nearby, so as not to have witnesses of their criminal and dirty activity. They beat our brother in faith Titov Daniil until he lost consciousness, and in this state they threw him in a car . . . They stopped the movement of the electric trains until the end of this operation. The arrests continued also at the station. 30 persons were arrested in all.

"To show the magnitude of this shameful, illegal revenge, the central railway station on Kiev, where those who escaped came, was surrounded by an armed regiment of police, a few buses with military forces, and the workers of the KBG. (The explanation is that the authorities knew about the sympathies of the population for the Underground Church. My note) . . . On the next day, that is, the 23rd of May, the believers decided at the end of their work period to go to the general attorney of the republic with a complaint. But the believers were not allowed to see the attorney; not even to enter the building of the attorney — this being surrounded with policemen. That whole part of the town of Kiev was surrounded with a great number of secret policemen. (Again a sign of the sympathy of the population for the Underground Church, about which the authorities knew.) Under these circumstances, the believers were obliged to return and to gather in the house of the brother in faith, G. S. Maghel, to pray.

"After 15 minutes, many buses of the police, headed by the same General-Major Detiarev, came to this house. They began to remove the believers in groups from the house, to photograph and register them, and to take them in special cars to the preventive prison.

"A great number of people came together to see these things. So to give to his illegal actions a legal aspect and also to stir up in the people hatred and bitterness against the faithful, the leader of this operation, the aforementioned General-Major, delivered to the people a provocative, slandering speech in which he depicted the believers as criminals against the state, whoremongers, thieves, drunkards and murderers, mentioning cases of kidnapping AND KILLING OF CHILDREN and giving the impression to the people that such things were the work of the faithful. (Just as in Nero's times the Christians were accused of setting fire to Rome and to have poisoned wells, and as the Jews have been accused of ritual murders.) At the end of his speech, he said, without any logic, these words: 'Citizens, beware for your children. The statistics prove that in recent time the juvenile criminality has increased.'"

From the speech it can be seen what this man and those who have rights and authority, and who gave the order for this unprecedented revenge, are capable of.

As a result of this last shameful operation, 100 persons were arrested in two days ... During the inquiry, tortures were used against some of the Christians. It is also known, that against some of the faithful (who for this cause got only 15 days of prison) some criminal charges were made.

"Besides this, the men of the Secret Police pursue Christians now in the town of Kiev, in secret as well as public dogging of the houses and persons of the believers. Some are simply hunted."

The representative authority of Kiev and the one entrusted by the Soviet for questions of religion, Comrade Sihonin, declared that all these measures of moral, economic, and physical action will be continued until the believers either cease to believe in God or else join the congregations led by the official leaders of the Baptists (who are stooges of the Communists). "And all this happens not in some backward colonial country or under a Fascist regime, it happens in a country which for 50 years has said to the whole world that it built the most just, democratic, and truly human society which declares the equality of all men, independent of race and religious attitudes."

By all we have exposed above, it can be seen that all Communist declarations and slogans are only a show intended to deceive their own people and the international public. In reality, it is very clear that the Communist Party of the Soviet Union, as a party of atheists, has made the decision to create in our country such conditions for believers that they will not be able to witness for their faith, or, even to live. Their purpose is the physical extermination of the believers.

"After the 23rd Congress of the Communist Party of the Soviet Union, this decision has been declared publicly, and the work for 're-education' by force of the believers is carried out in a centralized, well thought out and organized manner."

The President of the Executive Committee of the District Privoljskii, who has the name of Kazani, declared to the believers, "I can deliberately send some children to your worship service and then put you in prison because you have attracted children in your church." This latter episode is taken from a letter signed by the representative's Underground Church in the town of Ioshkr-Ola.

Lithuania is a country which has been stolen by the Communists. It is considered that they have killed or deported from this little country, over 1,300,000 men. Even now, 175,000 Lithuanians, among whom are many priests and bishops, are living in Siberian concentration camps. Of 16 bishops which this country had before, only three are alive now, and two of them are forbidden to leave their apartment. Out of the 1,099 churches which existed in this country before, half have been transformed into theaters, dancing halls, and auditoriums. Lithuania once had 4 large seminaries with 600 students. Now they have one sole seminary with 23 students. All the monasteries have been closed. The churches are not allowed to teach the children anything about faith.

Pravda Vostoka, of the 22nd of December, 1966, writes about the trial against the Protestant Christians Hrapov, Hartfeld, Matiohiha, and Bohn. Before the court trial, a reporter interviewed them and the Christians declared, "We suffer for our faith." These are members of the "illegal" Baptist organization in the town of Tashkent. Hrapov is the leader of this organization for all south Asiatic Russia. He had been three years in prison already, but immediately after having been released resumed his underground work.

One of the charges against this Protestant is that he printed and distributed secretly a magazine called *The Herald of Salvation*. A charge was brought that this magazine contained the following sentences: "Every scientist is powerless, is nothing before his Creator; before his Creator he is a worm" ... "An authority which gives un-Christian orders can't be recognized by a Christian as an authority from God." ... "The whole people of God must rise in the fight against sin, attack and don't fear." This organization had its own secret printing press. The newspaper says they did especially dangerous work among the children who, as a result of hearing the Gospel, "ceased to wear the red necktie of the Communists."

In the town of Kazan there is a great asylum for madmen in which there exists no true madman, but thousands of political prisoners detained without sentence in this form. The Soviets boast about their liberty, so if they dislike somebody they very often, rather than putting him in prison, declare him to be insane. Many thousands are put in this asylum because of their Christian faith. *Ucitelskaia Gazata* of November, 1962, itself acknowledges that they have put in the asylum for madmen eighty-two Christians, out of whom *26 died after a few weeks because of prolonged prayers.* Think about your brethren in strait jackets and gagged! The Soviets admit themselves that they behave like this with Christians.

Radio Riga of the 4th of June, 1965, announced that from a couple of Christians their three children have been taken away because "their souls were spoiled by indoctrination with religious superstitions." Thousands of such cases happen continually in the Soviet Union.

"Zvigne Riga" of July of last year announced that the church of St. Simanis in the town of Valmiera, has been made into a club. This has happened also with Dome of Riga. Twelve thousand inhabitants of the town of Valmiera are thus without a church.

Of some 300 Lutheran churches which existed in Latvia in 1939, only 110 were open in 1963, and since then others have been closed. In the Latvian district of Grovinas, out of 25 parishes and as many pastors there remains 10 parishes with 6 pastors. Has any one of you ever heard of the Lutheran bishop of Latvia, who is recognized by the Lutheran Federation and the World Council of Churches as "a real bishop," protesting against this ignominy?

The only literary form admitted in the Soviet Union is that called "Socialist Realism." They understand by this that the literature must not mirror exceptional men in exceptional circumstances, but the average reality in the world. Therefore, when you see a Soviet film and when you read their novels, you get a mirror of the realities. This mirror, in a certain measure, magnifies what is beautiful and diminishes or passes into silence what is wrong in the Soviet reality, but always the facts are taken out of reality.

Now, it is very interesting to find in the May, 1966, issue of the magazine *Science and Religion*, which appears in Moscow, a novel. The title of the part of the novel published in this magazine is "Podpole" (the Underground). In this novel the writer describes the Underground Church in Russia in a literary form, taking, as might well be expected, an attitude against it.

In this novel, a certain Christian with the name of Elisha has the good idea to create schools for young Christians where they will have to learn the word of God. New preachers will also be prepared "who will be ready to suffer for the true faith."

The author, who has the name of Lav Ovalov, describes the secret printing of leaflets, a description of which we have also in secret records smuggled out of Russia. The Soviet newspapers also know of the existence of such printing presses, and tell about the sentencing of Christians for having worked at them.

The Christians who work in the Underground Church have in the yards of their houses very good dogs which warn beforehand if somebody approaches the house. Whosoever is a real brother knows the words of recognition which must be pronounced before getting an entrance to the house. They are from the one side, "In the name of the Father and the Son and the Holy Ghost," and from the other side, the answer comes, "Amen." If anyone knocked at the door who did not know the word of recognition, then the Christians, already persecuted by the authorities, disappeared somewhere underground or in the attic or in all kinds of hidden places which were prepared in a very inventive and clever manner. "There were double walls and some hidden places over which potatoes were put."

The organization of the Underground Church was a very strict one with very different ranks, the head of which was chosen once in every few years. All free time was used for writing letters, for making sermons, and for "calling upon believers to prepare themselves for the conflict with the Anti-Christ and his servants."

The young believers were given two great rules: to be silent, and to pray.

The young believers were told that all evil persons will be punished.

The atheist magazine describes the teaching in the secret seminary for young Christians. It is deep in the wood, many miles from any house, and at a distance from the last village over which you could pass only through mire and jungle such as which never man has passed over in Northern Siberia; there was the seminary! There were two houses, one for men and one for women. The houses were made out of wood. Even though it was in the forest, they made the houses so low and took such measures of caution that if you passed very near them you could not recognize that it was an inhabited place. The teachers were two women called Feodola and Iraida. The first one had been an illiterate farm woman until she learned as a member of the Christian church to read and write. But now nobody could surpass her in the knowledge of the Word of God. Iraida, the other professor, had finished a pedigogical institute. The Christians called this seminary "The Academy in the Forest." The magazine laughs about the secretary of the organization of the Communist youth of that district who had not the slightest idea of the existence of the seminary. But even the Christians only knew about it if they had something directly to do with the seminary, the rules of the conspiracy being kept perfectly.

Uncontestable documents prove this article in *Science and Religion* to be more than simple fiction. I have before me a letter smuggled out from a Northern Siberian prison. It is written by a Christian who was sentenced for a May, 1966, demonstration before a building of the Central Committee of the Communist Party in Moscow. The letter is dated 21 December, 1966. In the letter the writer tells about the trial before the tribunal of those arrested for the demonstration. When the judge scorned the Bible, our brother said, "Mr. Judge, may I ask you a question? How is it that the manure of rabbits has the form of a pellet, the manure of a horse the form of an apple, and the manure of a cow that of a pancake, and so on?" The judge said, "I could not answer such a question." And then our brother, who is now in a North Siberian prison said, "You know nothing about manure and you dare to laugh about the Word of God." The same judge laughed about the fact that in the Russian Bible the expression is used, "Abraham gave birth to Isaac." To this our brother answered that the great Russian writer Gogol, in his renowned novel *Taras Bulba,* uses the same expression when he says to his son, "I have given you birth and I will kill you." In this manner our brother dispensed with the stupid remarks of the Communist judge.

This brother made such an impression upon generals, members of government and very high personalities of the Soviet leadership, whose names we do not mention, but who came to prison to speak with him, that his interrogator said to the brethren of Moscow who inquired after him, "David Davidovici is a true Christian." Our brother writes that he observed that his interrogator's conscience was most disturbed about the role he had to play. In his beautiful letter smuggled out from the Siberian slave labor camp, he states that now there are dark clouds over the people of God, yet the Word of God tells us that when the clouds are full they give rain. Noah and his family had no need to fear the clouds of the flood. The more so we, who are in a better ship than theirs, have no need to fear.

All Soviet authorities have to use terror; they have no other means to defeat religion. In the December, 1965, issue of *Science and Religion*, they describe what happened in the town of Tambov. The reporter of the magazine first visited the house of political education and met the comrades there who were in charge of the atheistic fight. "These gave an oath in the name of Christ God that thanks be to God, the atheistic propaganda goes very well in their town and that they deliver many atheistic lectures." The same reporter went to visit the churches, saying that in their yards he could see not only old men and women as the atheists expect to see, but also persons that he did not expect to see. You could easily distinguish many youths. There were young boys and young girls. There were even children of the first grades of school. The reporter reports what the minister said to the girls and boys. "Be obedient to your teachers, don't beat other boys, behave in a decent manner with girls!" Such advice was surely very dangerous for the Communist state, so new atheistic measures for uprooting such a bad religion had to be taken. The article ends by saying that the great majority of the inhabitants of the town which he interrogated did not even suspect that an atheistic institution existed in the town. Tambovians believe in God, and terror is the only means by which the Communists can uproot such faith. After the article is finished there is a footnote from the magazine editors which says that the facts contained in that article are characteristic of many towns. The same things were true about the towns of Pskov, Kostroma and Vladimir.

Leonide Ilyitschev has written in the periodical *Communist* that "the war against religion should not be just another campaign, but a permanent task in the building of Communism, in which all public authorities must join." Ilyitschev is a prominent member of the Central Committee of the Communist Party of the Soviet Union, and all measures of terror are decided by this organ. *Pravda*, the Soviet Communist Party newspaper, announced that an institute of scientific atheism will be established to accelerate the complete elimination of religious prejudices. Anyone who knows the Soviets, and the depth of the faith of the Russian people, will realize that the elimination of that faith cannot be accomplished any other way than by terror.

Khrushchev boasted ten years ago about "not having one single political prisoner in the Soviet Union." We have the evidence that there are great slave labor camps for political prisoners as well as for those who suffer for their Christian faith. The *Chicago Tribune*, on the 8th of May, published a list of such labor camps, in which, according to their information, there were something like 250,000 war prisoners. We have information proving that these camps are not only for war prisoners, but also for Russians who oppose the regime on political and religious motives. Below we give the names of these camps:

Lumbovka, in which the prisoners work in factories and at the construction of freeways; Jaroslav, where prisoners construct a canal; Kameneac-Podolsk, where the prisoners build airports and freeways; Pervomaisk, where the prisoners work at a cement factory; Krivoi-Rog, where prisoners work in a cellulose factory and building freeways; Uka was mostly for women. The same in the prison camp of Ivashka. Kamtschatka, Kara-Kum, Karabash, in which the prisoners also work in factories and at the building of highways. In the district of the Baikal Lake, and on the river Amur, there are also several camps. Of these, we know of the camps of Bogosh, Komsomolska, Gandala, and Wangar. Here the prisoners raise the food, make airports, work in factories and build highways. In all these places there are still innumerable German, Hungarian, and Czech war prisoners, but also many thousands of Christians who suffer for their faith.

Pravda Ukraini publishes on the 4th of October, 1966, an article about the condemnation of Bundarenko, Velitshko, Overtshuk, Ketshik, and Jurilo. Their crime is that of having spread leaflets in which they asserted that to submit to the rules made by the Communists means for the church to miss the blessings of God. In the same leaflet they said, "In our day Satan dictates and the Church (meaning the official Baptist church led by stooges of the Communists), accepts every decision, even if it goes openly against the commandments of God." The leaflet continues by saying that as long as the church does not free itself from the Communist stooges, it cannot be blessed by God (a fact which is true also for America, not only for Russia). Another "crime" of those who appeared in this case before the tribunal was that they demanded full religious liberty. A charge against them was that they prevented the school age son of a Baptist who died from being buried in a Communist manner, by arranging instead for him a Christian burial. Another crime of theirs was to bring children to Christ. One of the witnesses of the prosecution charged that Brother Boradarenko said that parents must educate children in a religious spirit and youth must gather around Christ. The accused ones run secret Sunday schools for children between the ages of 5 to 14. These, our brethren, were sentenced to from 2 to 3 years in prison.

Sovietskaia Iustitsia, of May, 1964, describes also the secret meetings of believers in little rooms in which the Christians could not kneel because there was no place for kneeling, and where the light in the gas lamp was quenched because there was no more air in the room. There, the Pastor Subbotin committed the crime of saying in a sermon, "Trust in God from all your heart and don't rely on your reason" (a recommendation which I would give also to American Christians). His crime was aggravated by the fact that at this secret religious service there were also children.

In front of the house there were always a few of the Christians watching, so that they should not be surprised by the Communist authorities. The Communist newspapers say that, "Subbotin came before the desk of the judge powerfully and confident, defying the tribunal by his poise, wishing to prove to man by his behavior that because of his faith he was ready for every torture and privation."

The newspaper says in indignant words that prayers have been made late in the night in an illegal form (what is a legal and what is an illegal prayer?), in unhygienic conditions (they don't allow the Christians to have prayer houses; the Christians have to gather in small rooms and then they are charged to have gathered in unhygienic conditions!) A medical doctor appeared as a witness before the court to say that the room was too small for so many believers and their health endangered because of the bad air. The conclusion that was reached was not to give the Christians a greater prayer house, but rather, to condemn the Christians to five years of prison.

One of those sentenced to prison with Subbotin, a man with the name of Hmara, died a few weeks after having been sentenced. His corpse was given back to the family. The hands and feet were burned, the lower part of the belly was split, and the whole body was full of bruises.

The article finishes with the demand that the children of those who have been sentenced should be put in atheistic boarding schools where they will be brought up as "builders of Communism!"

I appeal to all the parents who read this book to try for a moment to imagine how they would feel if their children would be permanently taken away from them to be forever poisoned with the Communist religion of hatred.

Pravda Vostaka, of the 15th of November, reports about a trial in Namanagan that was a show trial against the Baptists. Show trials are trials which hundreds and sometimes thousands of workers from different factories, and children from schools, are obligated to attend. The defendant, Mary Shevtshiuk, was charged with having required her children to transcribe by hand parts of the Bible and Christian songs. The newspaper says, with a word of alarm, "that such activity can have dangerous results for the formation of the character and life conceptions of these children." The accused Tkatshenko was charged to have asserted that she had heard a song from heaven. (It didn't come into Herod's mind to jail the shepherds of Bethlehem who have made the same assertion. Brejnev is worse than Herod.)

Kazakstanskaia Pravda, of the 12th of December, describes a trial in the town of Semipalatinsk. The result of this trial has been that the Christians Kiwosheev and Rudnev have been deprived of parental rights. Their children have been taken away from them and put in an atheistic boarding school. Their parents are not allowed to visit them, but still have to pay the fees for their children. Imagine that somebody would pull your weeping children from your arms and drive them away forever in a van of the secret police!

Sovietskaia Kirghizia, from the 8th of December, reports the sentencing of Petersen Jacob, one of the leaders of the Baptists, to four years of prison.

All of those sentenced had their entire property confiscated, and the tribunal decided also to deport them after the prison sentence has been fulfilled.

We would never finish giving all the names and cases of sentencing of Christians between the years of 1962 and 1966.

Turkmenskaia Iskra, of the 7th of October, says that murderers destroy a man physically, whereas the Christians destroy them morally; so they have to be sentenced. One of the accused Christians, asked what he had to say about the fact that his children were taken away from him, answered: "In all may the will of God be accomplished."

Uchitelskaia Gazeta, of the 18th of June, charges that the family Mullin went so far that they even tried to escape with their children to another town in order to have the children not taken away from them.

In another issue of the same magazine we find the record of a Christian who, forced to choose whether to remain with his faith or to be deprived of his children, answered, "I give up my children in order to have God," an answer which reminds us of Abraham when he had to sacrifice Isaac. It is the literal fulfilling of the words of Psalm 45, which we in the West usually recite without taking them earnestly, "Harken, O daughter, and consider, and incline thine ear; forget thine own people, and thy father's house; So shall the king greatly desire thy beauty: for he is thy Lord; and worship thou Him."

Kazakstanskaia Pravda, of the 31st of January, describes a trial against Christians in Karaganda who have committed the crime of having won 200 souls for Christ. Because of this a show trial was made against them in the Culture Palace of the town. The defendents Drobkov, Domanskii, and others who had already been in prison for their faith, had committed the crime of composing Christian hymns. They had said that "God must have the first place in our souls, feelings, and deeds." They said that, "We must remain far out of the world because earthly life is transitory, whereas true life is in Heaven." One of the witnesses of defense, Alexei Kirko, said simply to the judges, "What you sow, you will reap." The director of the school, Molevskoi, recounted before the court that when the classes ended, the Christian children tore from their necks the red necktie which they were obliged to wear, and then began their second Christian life. At the trial, a medical professor spoke about the great harm which prayer brings to human organism, adding that these men must be sentenced for having done this harm. The article in the newspapers, after reporting that the Christians have been sentenced to 3 and 5 years in prison, says the earth does not burn yet under the feet of these fanatics, inciting people on to newer and more evil persecution.

The same newspaper tells about a mother who killed herself and her child in order to prevent his being taken to an atheistic boarding school and the loss of his soul.

Komsomalskaia Pravda, of the 22nd of May of the year 1964, tells a story of a child of 7 years called Yakola Sviridov, who was an example of Christian faith and always isolated himself for prayer. He was forcibly taken away from his parents and put in an atheistic boarding school. But here he continued to pray, so they put him in the house of the captain of the secret police, Hutorin, who required him to say that the gods are invented. But the Communist newspaper had doubts itself as to whether he meant the gods of Greek mythology about which he has been told, or the God in whom he believed. After the things which he has passed through, the newspaper tells us that he had the malady of miocarditis, a malady of the heart. When at last he saw his mother again he asked, "Who is this woman?" He did not recognize her.

Sovietskaia Rossia, of the 23rd of May, complains that in the Christian assemblies "Men kneel and arrive to ecstacy" (how good it would be for Western Christians to arrive to the same state when they kneel). They had also listened to sermons broadcast over the foreign radio. They had taped these sermons and had distributed the tapes; they had taught the Christian youth to spread propagandistic letters. The article says that the Christians "hunt with stubbornness the youth." The sentences were of 3 and 5 years.

Pravda Ukraini, of the 12th of July, 1966, has an article entitled "They Received What They Deserved," telling about the condemnation of Christians to 5 years of prison.

Sovietskaia Rossia speaks about the orthodox priest Turkovskii. He and his Christians attempted to prevent the youth from playing volleyball in the church yard during the time of the divine service, as the Communist youth had arranged. For this he was sentenced to four years of prison.

Komsomalskaia Pravda, of the 22nd of March, 1964, describes the horror of a teacher when she sees that 9 of the children are wearing crosses. The article says that we must compel the Christian children to read anti-religious books and to learn modern dances. Thus we save a man and bring him out of the dark underground. What the Communists hate the most is that sometimes the secret meetings of the Underground Church take place in the houses of the Communists, who are Communists only on the surface and in their hearts believe in God. They also help the Christians. So it happened in the town of Shushcinsk, as *Kazatstanskaia Pravda* reports on 17 May, 1962.

Sovietskaia Kirghizia, of November, 1966, speaks about the trial against Nina Bikova, who ran secret religious schools for children below 7 years of age. The children were told to keep the rules of the conspiracy, and they have kept them. The Communist newspaper itself says that only accidentally they have discovered the schools. In Russia even children know to be "wise as serpents" in the service of the Lord.

Komsomalskaia Pravda, of the 8th of December, 1966, describes an atheistic meeting in Tiraspol. At this meeting a Baptist is judged. He answers, "How can I have common language with you, the Communists, when that Communist curses? I tell him that this is ugly. He answers, 'Shut up. God forbids you to curse, he does not forbid me'."

Trud, December, 1966, describes again an underground meeting. The householders have hid the dog so that it will not bark. Christians watch around the house. In the house dinner is prepared so that if anyone enters by chance he should not know it is a secret prayer meeting. They speak very low. The

newspaper gives, with exclamations of horror, the names of young men between 15 and 21 years of age who attend this meeting.

All those who work in this way in the Underground Church ultimately
have to go to prison.

It is not enough for them to leave their faith to avoid prison. *Sovietskaia
Latvia,* of the 27th of June, 1964, says, "We have proposed to ourselves as
an aim not only to take men out of the influence of the church, but also to
transform them into militant atheists." Nothing less than this can satisfy the
Communists. It is not enough for them if you cease to worship, you must
begin to blaspheme God and Christ. That is the measure of the struggle in
Russia.

Selskaia Jizn, of the 13th of May, 1965, reports that in the collective
Rossia of the district Tutaevsk, two girls of the priest came to school with
crosses. They were told not to come to school any more.

The reactions of the Christians are as they were in the first centuries of
persecution.

Some have taken the attitude of passive resistance. So, for example, did
the sisters Volovnia in the town Uslovaia, where they entered into a hunger
strike, as *Isvestia* reports. The girls have answered to a reporter, "We are
ready to die for faith and justice."

Their mother said, "My daughters will fast until the persecution against
us from the side of the atheists is finished. If the persecution continues, they
will die." The hunger strike has been announced by leaflets which Christians
have put in the post boxes of all the houses of the towns. The leaflets said, "Full
liberty for the activity of Baptists or the death of our two sisters."

Other Christians take the way of armed violence. From 7 places it is reported that traitors and informers of the secret police who were smuggled
into the Underground Church only escaped with very great difficulty attempts
to punish them with death.

What bewilders the Communists, as *Pravda Vostoka* says the 29th of
February, 1964, is that the Christians who come before the tribunal are
generally considered as good and honest men, often rewarded for their ex-
emplary work.

The charges are in every case the same, to have listened to religious broad-
casting from abroad, to have reprinted foreign Christian literature, to have
demanded religious liberty, and to have tried to win children for Christ.

In Soviet Russia, to be a Christian means not only to go to prison, but to
show daily heroism. *Sovietskaia Rossia,* of the 27th of December, 1966,

describes how in the village Elan of the district of Volgograd, the president
of the collective calls upon the old woman Jukavskii to discuss with her the
repair of the roof of her house which is in poor condition. The old woman is
80 years of age. The president of the collective says she must leave the church.
She says she will not do so. Then the president of the collective answers, "May
the church repair your house! We will not do it." So the old sister of ours has
to remain in the ancient house in which rain and snow and dust enter freely.

In *Komsomalskaia Pravda*, the 5th of July, 1962, the very word "underground" is used. Different Christians are reported to have organized the Underground Church, a church in which they had to abstain from light; they had to
beware of the physical light in order to have the real light of the world.

Komsomalskaia Pravda, of 25th of September, 1962, characterizes the
Christians as men who teach hatred toward their fellow man, yet they admit
also the following two points: "We think sometimes of our Christian adversaries as stupid or crooks who wish to live on the charge of others. But Sheve-
cenko, who appeared before court, is an engineer and clever. He has already
been sentenced three times. He knows psychology and the rules of conspiracy.
He went from house to house." He, with a group of Christians, is accused of
burning the neckties of Pioneers and having trampled under their feet the red
flag, the flag red with the blood of Communists. This same article acknowledges that Christians work sometimes under the cover of the Communist
youth movements.

Sovietskaia Moldavia, of the 23rd of August, 1963, after reporting about
a Christian who has already been 9 years in prison, says, "Why are show trials
against the sectarians so rare in our villages and our towns, where there have
remained witnessing brethren and sisters in Christ? Are we not too soft with
them?" Articles like this tell us what we have to expect to happen in the future
to the Christians.

Sovietskaia Iustitsia, of May, 1964, speaks about children who multi-
plied by photocopying such slogans as "God is Love," or "Throw upon God
All Your Cares." They say that it is especially the youth which makes up the
Underground Church, about which some American church leaders have not
even heard. In some cases, the Christians are charged with refusing to participate in the comedy of elections, elections at which you have to say "yes" to
the only candidate of the Communist Party, and that they also refuse to pay
taxes to the Communist government.

Sovietskaia Iustitsia, of May, 1964, states that it must be considered a crime to bring minors to a religious service, even if they are the relatives of the accused ones. It is a crime not only to convert, but even to bring minors to an illegal religious meeting and to make them participate in religious prayers and religious ceremonies. The crime of spreading religious propaganda is considered perpetrated no matter how the citizens have reacted to it. So the simple fact is that if you invite a minor to a religious service, even if the minor does not come, you are considered a criminal.

Komsomalskaia Pravda, of April, 1963, also uses the expression "the Underground Church" (the existence of which is contested by some church leaders in America), and describes how the Christians gathered in specially-arranged hidden places.

A secret report from Russia speaks about a huge revival in Central Asiatic districts. In that area live the so-called Volga Germans, who were deported during World War II. They write: It seems that there has not been one corner in which the Holy Ghost has not looked in bringing souls to Christ. There have been awakened to a new life such men from whom you would not have expected it. Young men who drank yesterday and were very bad, witnessed the next day that Jesus had become their Savior. The young generation doesn't know the German language, so they can't read even the scarce German Bibles which they have. They don't know the songs either, but they prayed so in the Russian language that "even a stone would have been softened." During the summer of 1965, the revival passed to the children. They would sing from song books written by hand. The brother who writes the report asks, "Can you imagine what it means to write a whole hymn book by hand?" Here also many of the Christians became martyrs for having begun the protest against the persecution.

In this report we find for the first time the news that a renowned Russian writer, Boris Pasternak, around whose name there was so much noise a few years ago, when the Russian government forbid him to receive the Nobel prize, died as a converted man. He wrote a beautiful poem to the glory of Christ which ends with the words, "I have covered your feet Jesus, with tears, I have wrapped up your feet in my cloak, and then I have put my beads on your neck." (Could not also some American Christian sisters put their beads on the necks of the martyrs in the Communist camp, giving them away for their benefit? How beautiful is a Christian girl's neck without jewels, when these have been given away for such a purpose!) This is even more so "a sign of the time," as Boris Pasternak is of Jewish origin. Many of the leaders of the underground behind the Iron Curtain and many of the martyrs there are

Hebrew Christians. God chooses again a remnant of this people as Isaiah predicted.

In *Sovietskaia Moldavia,* of the 13th of August, 1966, there is an article bearing the title, "Where the Bells Rang." In this article we are told that in Valea Perjinskii the church was transformed into a museum. In the district of Novo-Anenskii, several churches were transformed into libraries, clubs, and so on. The same happened in the village Korjavo. In the Village Cretoaia, the church was transformed into a club, and many other such cases are known. In America many spread the lie that Communism is mellowing. The Communists themselves say otherwise. They close the churches today.

Our news given in this part of the book bears dates beginning with 1961, but the situation has never changed or mellowed.

Sovietskaia Rossia, of the 22nd of November, 1966, tells about the judgement against Bikova, Maiorova and others for the same crime of having brought children to Christ.

I have spoken until now mostly about the Protestant underground, but there exists also Catholic and Orthodox ones. The *Byzantine Catholic Word* reports on 29 August, 1965, about a secret religious publishing operation in Moscow. Several persons were arrested for operating a printing plant behind an electric light bulb factory. About 400 pounds of Catholic religious literature were confiscated. In related incidents it was reported that a man called Starykov was arrested at the Moscow Airport while preparing to take printed pictures of the Virgin Mary to Catholics in the Ukraine. This man succeeded in getting the printing director of the Institute of Agriculture Research to publish Orthodox prayer books, church calendars, and religious texts. *Pravda* said of this case that "These two persons chiefly responsible in the matter will be tried and Christian clemency need not be expected by them."

On the 22nd of January, 1967, an exhibition of art was opened in Moscow in which 11 artists participated. The show had been scheduled for Sunday, Monday and Tuesday, but it was closed after a single hour because the works exhibited carried strong religious motifs. One of the painters of Jewish origin, Oskar Rabin, exposed two pictures, one of the Virgin Mother and Child, and the other of Christ over a village in darkness. It was meant to show that only Christ and the Biblical persons can show you the right way. Another painting depicted century-old Slavic manuscripts of ancient origin. No art is permitted if it shows Christ.

Sovietskaia Rossia, of the 5th of August, 1966, says that during an inquiry made in the school 68 in Gorolovaka, they found out that religious children are characterized by a double life. They don't admit in school that they are Christians; they adapt themselves. They answer at lessons as they are meant to answer, because otherwise they would be expelled from school. But secretly they go to church, keeping in their pockets their red neckties. The children keep their faith, accommodating themselves to the circumstances of terror.

In *Komsomalskaia Pravda*, of 24th of September, 1965, a certain Mrs. Kelt writes that "closed parishes do not transform believers into atheists. On the contrary, it increases people's propensity to religion, and embitters their hearts besides."

We have in Russia a nadir of human brutality and a zenith of Christian heroism.

Sovietskaia Moldavia speaks about a pupil of the 7th degree, Kolia Cercel, who said simply to its reporter, "I believe everything which is written in the Bible. In the Bible everything is true." The newspaper adds that atheistic propagandists have no convincing arguments; there remains nothing else for the Communists than to practice terror.

By purpose, I have given all this material unsystematically, just at random as it appears from a pile of Soviet newspapers. Everyone who knows Russian and reads the Communist newspapers reads every day things such as those which we have reported here.

Now contrast this with the article of Karev, the General Secretary of the Official Baptist Union, a stooge of the Communists, who publishes in *Soviet Life* of June, 1963, the right of Baptist parents to raise their children in the spirit of faith, and who praises the Soviet humanism. Compare this with the praises given to Communist liberty by the World Council of Churches. The Archbishop Nikodem of Russia, the one who dictates in Geneva, says that religious liberty is guaranteed by the Soviet law, and that Russian churchmen "get indignant over the attempts of the champions of the cold war to distort the real picture of religion in our country." The same says that "relations between the church and state are supervised by government councils which are responsible to the Council of Ministers of the U.S.S.R. The main task of these councils is to see that the liberty of conscience is observed in our country and that all questions raised by the supreme church authorities are properly solved." (Current developments in the Eastern European churches, April, 1963.)

In an interview published by "Tass," the Soviet government news agency, Metropolitan Pimen, Vicar of the Patriarch, says Russian churches "have no reason for anxiety as the right to profess any religion or no religion at all is guaranteed in Article 124 of the Soviet Constitution." The same, infamous Nikodim says that in Russia there is no religious persecution, "but a struggle of ideas." Professor Shishkin of the Sociological Academy of the Russian Orthodox Church in Leningrad, another stooge of the Communists, deplores even the lack of rights of the atheists in the Soviet Union. He says, why is it that the Christians have so many means of propaganda, the reading at worship of the Word of God, the predication of sermons, the singing of religious hymns, and the administration of sacraments? Atheists can express an attitude to religion only through the spoken or written word. The poor atheists have no cult, no sanctuaries, no ministers. "It was the principle of freedom of conscience proclaimed in the country that required special stress in fundamental law and the right of Soviet citizens who are atheists to conduct anti-religious propaganda, otherwise the non-believers would be in a position of unequality compared to believers."

Christians are jailed en mass, are tortured and are killed. Children are taken away from Christian parents, and yet the World Council of Churches, by the mouth of Archbishop Nikodim and other rogues like him, praises the religious liberty in the Soviet Union, and the American and British church leaders embrace this Archbishop Nikodim as a true representative of Russian Christianity!

In Red China things are even worse than in Russia. Travelers recently arriving in Hong Kong from China have reported that special haircuts, leaving a shaved area in the form of a cross, have been administered to people as a shameful identification of Christians. Other Christians have been forced to sit in gutters when Communist enthusiasts pass by spitting on them and reviling them. Others have been marched through the streets on display as religious bad elements, enduring the shame and ridicule of the crowds which is heaped on them. Others have been savagely beaten. All the churches of Red China have been closed. All the Bibles that guards could seize have been burned. As far as we know by past evidence, imprisoned Christians have been mutilated. Ears, tongues, and legs have been cut from them; one said to have passed through this ordeal is Watchman Nee, the renowned Chinese Evangelical writer, who was already 12 years in prison.

These American church leaders, who cry loudly for the admission of Red China to the organization of the United Nations, have not said one word of protest about their Christian brethren in Red China, this, of course, supposing the American side is constituted really of brethren in Christ.

In Rumania, the brethren at the time of this writing, Nailescu, Ghelbegeanu, Balauta, Alexandru, Gabrielescu, are still in prison, and so are very many others.

In Hungary there are still concentration camps in which Christians are detained. Some 60,000 Hungarians who have been deported to Siberia during the revolution, have never been brought back.

This is the real situation of Christianity behind the Iron Curtain, *and it cannot be contradicted,* and whosoever says otherwise lies to the American people.

Again, I say, the facts shown by me cannot be contradicted!

EPILOGUE

The words of the Bible which I like most are in John, Chapter 13, "Jesus having loved his own which were in the world, he loved them unto the end."

I have spoken in this book about the crimes of the Communists. I have spoken also about the equal crime of complying with them and helping them to take over the free world. I have spoken about the crime of remaining deaf to the cries of suffering of the Church behind the Iron Curtain.

What will our attitude be toward those who commit these crimes?

It can be only one of love. A Christian should hate sin and love sinners. A Christian should hate the cruel dictatorship of militant atheism, he should hate Communist exploitation and oppression. But he should love the man and he should love his church leaders who, some consciously, others duped, help these enemies of Christ to conquer. Jesus loved his enemies and asked for their forgiveness when nailed to the cross. Jesus loved Judas, too, and called him "friend" when he came together with soldiers to arrest him in the Garden of Gethsemane.

Our hearts are framed in such a manner as not to love well. We always disappoint those who have given us their love. But the love of God is not dependent upon our behavior towards him. It is unconditioned, it is the expression of his unmoving character. He loves to the end, and all those who are children of God and partakers of the divine nature love like him. It is easy for them to love even their torturers, and to love also those who praise their torturers.

For us it is easy to love because we know the Word of God. In the book of Revelation, Chapter 7, we read that one of the elders said, "What are these which are arrayed in white robes? and whence came they?" The answer is, "These are they which came out of great tribulation, and have washed their robes, and made them white in the blood of the Lamb." The Communist torturers and killers, as well as their accomplices in the Western church have helped the Christians behind the Iron Curtain to pass through tribulations and to be now arrayed in white robes for which angels could envy them. We have lost nothing permanent by our sufferings. Those who truly lose are the Communists and those who help them. We pity those and we would like to be helpful to these.

The modern Cains have prepared for us prison cells and chains, but in these prison cells with 50 pounds of chains at their feet, Christians often felt like they were in the Garden of Paradise. They walked again with God as the first Adam, for chains prevent nobody from walking with God.

In the Soviet camp thousands have died and are dying for the sake of Christ. Many of them are very young. I have seen boys die the death of martyrs, young men of 17 and 18, and my wife has seen young girls die. But when a man becomes a saint in his old age he sacrifices to God only the devil's leavings. With us youth knows to give to God as a holy sacrifice their bodies. They are now glorified saints in Heaven. They have loved to the end. The more so we who have not had the privilege to get a martyr's crown should love like this.

But love is only one of the Christian virtues. There exists the virtues of righteousness and of common sense, which teach us to do what is practical in order to help the enslaved people in their churches.

I come from the Communist world, and I write and speak mostly about Communism, but I am not obsessed with the Communist problem. Wesley has said "The whole world is my parish," and I could say the same thing about myself. Many of the Western church leaders are guilty not only of neglecting the suffering Christians behind the Iron Curtain, they are guilty of neglecting their duties toward the whole world. I could say that in some ways the situation of the church behind the Iron Curtain is much less alarming than that of the church in the West. In England the number of those who go to church is decreasing continually. At Easter 1966 only three per cent of the population of London attended a religious service. In Great Britain, of each thousand of children who go to Sunday school, only 27 become afterwards members of the church. In the whole of Scandinavia the percentage of those who attend regularly church services is something around 5 per cent. Have you seen your church leaders very concerned about this?

We believe about certain organizations that they are big and seem to represent many people. In reality, these organizations are insignificant. So, for example, the Church of England is represented and has a great voice in the World Council of Churches, but the Church of England really does not exist. Even Westminster Abbey, the great cathedral of London, is empty on Sunday mornings and so are most of the other Anglo-Catholic churches. There exists an Evangelical party within the church, but this is usually opposed to the World Council of Churches. The Archbishops who go to Geneva represent empty churches, and so it happens with many other countries too.

Many of the Western church leaders are shepherds who don't care for their own flocks, and it may seem naive from my part to have asked from them to care for the persecuted flock behind the Iron Curtain.

But now I don't speak any more to them. I speak to you, the rank and file Christian and pastor. You must know the truth which your leaders hide from you.

Lenin wrote in his 15th Volume, "The Marxist must be a materialist, it is an enemy of religion." The enmity between Marxism and Christianity is as fundamental as the enmity between God and Satan, and between sin and righteousness.

Communists, as long as they remain Communists, can never be something else than mass torturers and mass killers of Christians, and mass poisoners of children and youth with atheism.

The blood of the killed brethren and the blood of the children whose souls will be lost because of the atheism which they have been taught, will be on your church leaders which have complied with Communism. But will it be only on them? Will it not be on you, too?

There exists a fashion with certain Christian circles in America to speak against the World Council of Churches and the National Council of Churches and other church leaders. Some feel that it is sufficient to hold meetings in America in which they speak out against Communism. I consider that to light a candle is always much more important than to curse the darkness. We surely must speak out against the treacherous attitude of church leaders. Surely the American people must be told the true horrors of Communism. The first book of the Bible says that the seed of the woman (by this the Savior is meant) "will bruise the head of the serpent." But so far we tickle the serpent on the belly and make him laugh, instead of bruising his head.

The head of the serpent is not in America, he is in Moscow, in Peiping, in Bucharest, and in Warsaw. Communism must be defeated there and not here, as Hitlerism had to be defeated by conquering Berlin.

Now there exists within these Communist countries a great power which, with the help of God, will overthrow Communism. It is the great power of the Underground Church. As I have shown in my book *Today's Martyred Church Tortured for Christ*, and in a former chapter of the present book, the Soviets themselves are alarmed about the quick growth of this Underground Church. That is what compels them to take such measures of terror against it. Yet terror is powerless against God, and the Underground Church will conquer them if it is helped by the American Christians.

The Underground Church behind the Iron Curtain does not fear the Communists because it has on its side God, and the great bulk of the free people.

In Russia, an ex-priest who had betrayed the Church, delivered an atheistic lecture and raised many arguments against Christianity. In the end a Christian stood up and said, "Comrade lecturer, you have avowed yourself that you have deceived us in times before when you were a priest, so you are not a trustworthy person even now. We will leave everything which you have said and we will instead pray." He turned to the audience, all bowed their heads, and after the Orthodox manner they sang together one of the hymns which is always sung at the Orthodox Liturgy. With this the atheistic meeting was finished! Things like this happen constantly in the Soviet Union, and they happen in the other Communist countries, too! The Underground Church is courageous and can overthrow Communism.

There can be no question of anything else than overthrowing Communism.

Lenin said in his 13th Volume on page 90, "A million sins, bestialities, rapes, and infections of a physical kind are more easily seen through by the crowd, and therefore less dangerous than the refined, spiritualized idea of God decked out in the most gorgeous costumes. The more refined and critical theology becomes, the more socially enticing and dangerous it becomes."

In America the Communists speak about dialogue with the Catholics and the Protestants, and some declare their sympathy especially with liberal theology. In the Communist countries the liberal theologians went to prison exactly as the fundamentalist ones. The Communists accept not the slightest notion of God. Who reads well the words of Lenin sees that he considered religion being much more dangerous than syphilis, cancer, and gangsterism, hooliganism, and so on.

Never can any church leader who loves Christ ever think about anything else than that the power of anti-Christ must be overthrown, and that we must join hands with those behind the Iron Curtain, who after 50 years of terror, still defy the oppressors and fight against them.

Lenin, in his book, *What Is To Do,* written in 1903, asked the Communists to exploit the persecution of the Protestant sects, and the Communists really exploited this persecution for their revolutionary purposes. The adversaries of Communism are not as wise as the children of this world. The Communists used the wrong done by the Czarist authorities against Protestantism for their purposes. America doesn't use this persecution of Christians for propagating the cause of freedom and we don't even publish the facts!

Bonch-Bruevich, one of the founders of the Bolshevik Party, said in the 2nd Congress of that party, when it fought in illegality against Czarism, that "the Protestant sectarians are an advanced and self-conscious sector of the mass." And in the same report he proposes, "We should endeavor through the sectarians to reach the vast peasant masses with our revolutionary propaganda." The Communists had this cleverness. They knew that the Protestant sectarians represent the tens of millions of peasants of Russia. They knew that the Protestant sectarians are the self-conscious part of the majority of the Russian people and tried to reach these masses by the sectarians for their revolutionary propaganda, although without success. We could learn from the Communists, and all those who oppose Communism should do their utmost to sustain the Underground Church behind the Iron Cutain.

The Communists have the power to kill Christians. The Christians have the power to give their lives away and not to fear, but to be thankful to be able to die for Christ. The one who dies gladly for a high cause is always more powerful than the one who can only kill. The blood of the martyrs has always been the seed which has made the Church grow.

Given time, the Underground Church will conquer.

But the Western church must also learn something. The first book of the New Testament was written some 40 years after the ascension to Heaven of our Lord Jesus Christ. The whole New Testament has been completed only around the end of the 1st century. What did the Christians of the first 40 years after the Resurrection of Jesus read? What was their Holy Book? They had a very Holy Book which is unknown to American Christians. This book was the living example of men like St. Stephen, and St. James, and many others who died as martyrs for Christ. Their examples were taught in churches. Their examples inflamed the hearts of younger Christians. Their examples made the Church to flourish. American Christians swim in Bibles but many don't really know this Holy Book, "the book of the martyrs of today, their lives, their sacrifices." Their answers before the judges should be published everywhere, and it should be made clear to the American Christian that the martyr in Russia and China and Rumania fights not only the fight of Christ, but also the fight for saving America from the menace of Communism.

I know that it is useless to preach and to write books when by your sermons and your books you only scratch men where it does not itch. Another's toothache or headache will never be very great concern for you. But the fight which is happening behind the Iron Curtain between the Underground Church and the anti-Christ is not another's headache. It is the only fight which can save America from the Communist menace.

Yet your political leaders (and some church leaders) have said that they don't have even the wish to overthrow Communism in other countries. They are Christians and say the "Our Father." Now in this prayer; they ask "Thy kingdom come." But how can the kingdom of God come if you don't overthrow the kingdom of Satan? How could the Republicans come to power in America if you don't overthrow the Democrats? How can the Democrats come to power if you don't overthrow the Republicans? And if another group wants to come to power they have to overthrow both. The one who really wishes that the kingdom of God will come must overthrow Communism.

But now the simple fact is that your responsible political leaders, for certain reasons, don't wish to overthrow Communism. And as long as Communism will not be overthrown, America will not be safe. One-third of the world and more will remain in the hands of men who declare themselves that their great aim is to put the red flag on the White House. There remains one single force which wishes to overthrow the Communist regime. This force is the Underground Church behind the Iron Curtain, and not only every Christian in America but every American patriot must be behind this force.

Therefore there exists only one possibility to avoid the Communist revolution in America. That is to cause a revolution in the thinking of Americans and American churches themselves. They must know that the principal foe for America is Communism, and how they must join hands with those who fight against this foe.

A pastor should never preach or write something else than the Gospel. The Greek word translated in English "Gospel" means in the original "Good News." In this book I have also preached the Gospel because I have given you good news. America is not lost yet. There exists a power behind the Iron Curtain which can save America. There exists a power behind the Iron Curtain which has not been broken by the Communist oppressors. There exists in the 20th century saints and heroes in faith just like those in the beginning of Christianity. Christianity has kept its vigor and its first love, the Bride of Christ shows again her radiant beauty.

What I have given is the Gospel because it is very good news.

Oh, that the spirit of the martyred church behind the Iron Curtain should pass to American Christianity!

In 1966 the authorities of Communist Rumania decided to close the church of St. Basil in the town of Oradea. Thousands of Christians filled this great church and surrounded it from all sides. They stood vigil in and around it, day and night, never allowing the authorities to approach it until the authorities abandoned their criminal project. How wonderful it would be if members of some American churches in which the leaders compromise with Communism, would do the same if they would fill and surround the churches and say "We will never leave these places until things change, until you join hands with the martyrs in the Communist camp, until you help them and take a firm stand against Communism!"

How wonderful it would be if your church leaders would receive millions of letters in which you would tell them "we give every year in our church, so and so much money, and we ask an accounting from you as to how much of what we give goes to the families of Christian martyrs behind the Iron Curtain (because we know perfectly there are such martyrs)!" How wonderful it would be if American Christians would ask their church leaders: "What are you doing for spreading secretly the Gospel in countries where the Gospel is forbidden?" How wonderful it would be if American Christians arose from their apathy and asked their church leaders to break any relationship with the Communist stooges who come from the East to the World and the National Council of Churches! How wonderful it would be if they would ask from their church leaders an unceasingly firm stand against the mass torturers and the mass killers of the Christians."

I, from my side, think that the example of Jesus, who drove out the merchants from the temple, must be repeated in America. And that all those who dare praise the killers of Christians from the pulpit should be driven out forever from the leadership of churches.

If you don't do this we will continue to go to church having forgotten the aim for which this church exists. God has created the church in order to oppose evil in all its forms in this world, and to proclaim the Kingdom of God. There is no bigger evil in the world today than Communism. Hitler appears as an innocent child in comparison with the Communist leaders. He has killed six million Jews, that was all. But what about Stalin, for his comrades said he has killed thirty million of men? Millions have been killed by Mao Tse Tung, Ceaushescu, and all the other Communist leaders. Any church which does not oppose them does not fufill the aim for which it has been created.

I am attending now so often church services in America, and I have the constant impulse when the pastor gives the benediction at the end to shout to him, "But pastor, you have not yet had the religious service." Every religious service at which the martyrs are not even mentioned, in which a prayer is not offered that God will strengthen their faith, is a divine service which is not valid before God.

In Catholic churches the martyrs are always mentioned, but only the martyrs of centuries ago. Those of today, who remembers them?

When visiting the zoological garden in San Diego, I was told that the Canadian geese which they have there have their wings cut and, therefore, can't fly back to their homeland, but they always go to the Northern fence of the place where they are detained, and are standing day and night by this fence, looking toward the North toward which they would like to fly if they only could. Every Christian is a man who wishes again to be with God, to be from where our souls come, to be with Jesus, our Heavenly Bridegroom. Every Christian wishes the establishment of the Kingdom of God. This is our highest dream. But Christ has said that first the Gospel of the Kingdom must be preached to all the nations and then the end will come. If you wish to be forever in the embrace of Christ, you must see that the Gospel is preached in all the nations. In one-third of the world a regime of terror hinders the spreading of the Gospel. No compromise with this regime of terror must be permitted.

The American Christians have neglected their duty to the Underground Church behind the Iron Curtain. I trace this thing of neglect to ignorance of the facts. In my book *Today's Martyred Church Tortured for Christ,* and the present one, I give uncontestable facts so no one will have a further excuse for ignorance. The secret of the right attitude is right knowledge. Now you have the right knowledge, and now I expect from every one an immediate change of attitude.

One-third of the world is enslaved by the Communists. This should be at least one-third of our concern, one-third of our sermons, one-third of our gifts in church, one-third of our prayers. This must begin immediately!

One of the greatest personalities of Christian life in America wrote to me that he will never lift a finger against Communism. Not to lift a finger against Communism means not to lift a finger on behalf of the victims of Communism. Don't you remember the words of Jesus that "You have not visited me when I was in prison, you have not cared for me when I was hungry and thirsty, you have not cared for me often as you did not do these things to my little brethren?" Those who suffer behind the Iron Curtain are the little brothers of Jesus, and it is an incredible shame for a Christian leader to say he will not lift a finger against those who torture a Christian.

In times of old the church had other leaders. In the 12th century in Britain, reigned the unjust king, Henry Plantagnet. Thomas Becket, at that time the Archbishop of Canterbury said: "The more important and fierce the prince is the stronger stick and harder chain is needed to bind him and keep him in order." He was cut down with swords, but the result has been that Plantagenet, after having killed Becket, was converted, and made pilgrimages to the shrine of the martyred Archbishop. Communists and even their rulers would be converted if Christianity would have again church leaders like this. And if the church leaders are not like this, then I expect the rank and file Christians and pastors to put aside their bad leaders and take themselves the leadership of their church in their hands.

One of the most dramatic moments of my life has been the following.

I was in prison with one of the greatest murderers of Rumania named Brandabura. When I asked him how many men he had killed he answered, "I never counted them." Even in prison he was always kept with chains at hands and feet because he was like a wild beast. If a guard told him a bad word he simply threw a stone at him. You could not keep him quiet.

I was once at the gate of the prison together with this Brandabura.

A van of the secret police stopped before the prison gate and out came a new transport of prisoners, among them the son of Brandabura, who was a murderer too, also sentenced to lifelong imprisonment. As father and son met at the prison gate the son lifted his chained hands toward his father and said, "Is it for this that you have procreated me?" And this father for the first time showed a sign of humanity. He bowed his head and blushed. You also have procreated children. The word to procreate is a very significant word, meaning that we are deputy creators. We create on behalf of God eternal beings, and you are responsible for the future destiny of these beings.

You Americans have gotten from your predecessors a beautiful inheritance. If you give up this inheritance, if you allow Communism to conquer the world and to conquer America too, after 20 to 30 years your children will lift toward you their chained hands and ask you, "Father, Mother, is it for this that you have brought me into the world?" And then in eternity in Hell, in the existence of which I believe with all my heart, your children will ask you, "Father, Mother, why have you given me birth and then not seen that I should be brought up in a society with the fear of God and the knowledge of the Savior?"

The destiny of the world and the eternal fate of your children is at stake in the problems which I have put in the present book.

Join hands this very moment with the Underground Church behind the Iron Curtain!

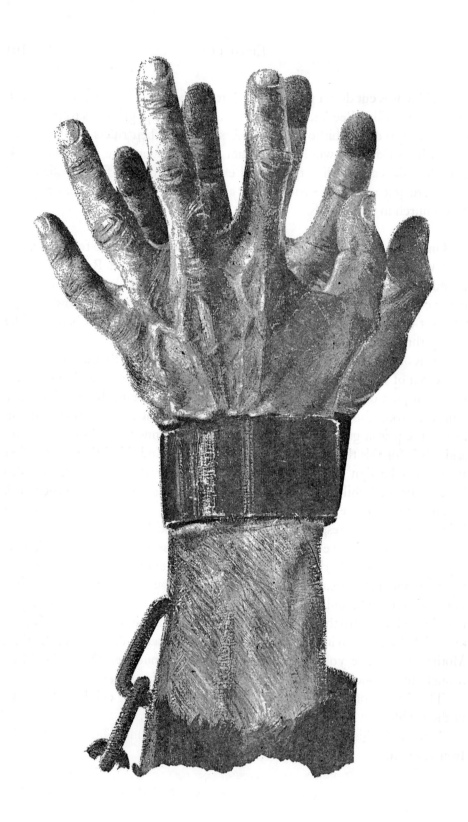

IMPORTANT DOCUMENTS CONFIRMING THE LIE

APPENDIX
TRANSLATION (French)
[TRANSLATOR'S NOTE: Since this material is a re-re-translation, a literal translation from the French is given below — so as not to lose any more of the flavor of the original text (Chinese).— EH.]

"LI WEI HAN" DOCUMENT

Important documents are lost in the succession of daily events.

"DIFFUSION — INFORMATION DOCUMENTAIRE" makes a point of furnishing tests in the form of pamphlets, presenting one document at a time.

Full translation of a document published in 1959 by: "The Foreign Language Press [Publications] of Peking for the use of the Latin American section of the Liaison Department of the Chinese Communist Party."

This document defines, in its own words, the [various] development stages of the "dialectical struggle within religion for the purpose of progressively replacing the religious element therein by the Marxist element, * * * and of leading the Catholics to destroy, by themselves and on their own account, the divine images which they themselves had created."

PUBLISHED BY THE FOREIGN LANGUAGE PRESS OF PEKING FOR THE EXCLUSIVE USE OF THE LATIN AMERICAN SECTION OF THE LIAISON DEPARTMENT OF THE CHINESE COMMUNIST PARTY

Printed in the People's Republic of China

THE CATHOLIC CHURCH AND CUBA
(ACTION PROGRAM)

The Catholic Church, which has its headquarters in Rome, is a reactionary organization which stirs up counter-revolutionary activities within the People's Democracies. So that the People's Democracies may continue to advance via Socialism and Communism, it is necessary, first of all, to do away with the influence of the Catholic Church and with the activities which it carries on. The Catholic Church is neither sterile nor impotent; on the contrary, its power must be recognized and a number of measures must be taken to block its way.

When the political struggle and the production forces have attained a high level of production [rate of productivity] it will be possible to destroy it [the church]. That is the objective to be attained and that is what we are fighting for. To make a frontal attack and to strike [it] in the face, as we will be poorly equipped and as we will not have educated the masses properly, would result only in giving the Church an even greater control over the masses because they would then feel in sympathy with it and clandestinely support its counter-revolutionary activities. It must also be prevented that the counter-revolutionary leaders of the Church would appear as martyrs. The line of action to be followed against the Church consists in instructing, educating, persuading, convincing, and gradually awakening and fully developing the political consciousness of the Catholics through obtaining their participation in study groups and political activities. We must undertake [engage in] the dialectical struggle within religion through the instrumentality of "activists" (militant Communists).[1] We will progressively replace the religious element by the Marxist element, gradually change the false consciousness into a true consciousness, so that the Catholics will eventually destroy of their own accord and on their own account, the divine images which they themselves had created. That is our line of action in the struggle for victory against the counter-revolutionary Catholic Church.

Furthermore, we will present a program of tactics applied with success in the Chinese People's Republic in order to liberate the Chinese people from the influence of the Imperialist Catholic Church of Rome.

The Church and its faithful must be induced to take part in the People's government so that the masses may exert their influence on them. The Church cannot be permitted to preserve its supra-national character which places it above the will of the masses. Within the People's government a Bureau in charge of religious affairs and organizations must be created. By imposing on the Church the processes of Democratic centralism the road is being opened through the instrumentality of the masses, to patriotic measures which will weaken the Church and reverse its prestige. This Bureau will organize national, regional, and local associations which will group the Catholics into patriotic organisms. Each association will manifest its submission to the laws of the nation, and its will to observe them.

When these associations have been created and have professed their submission to the laws of the nation, that is when the reactionaries and counter-revolutionists will come forth. These counter-revolutionists, risen from within the Catholic Church, are the first to be rooted up with determination, without, however, the use of force. In any event, the measures taken must be in accordance with the law. Counter-revolutionary aspirations, by their very nature, lead to actions against the government. This principle indicates to us what kind of laws must be applied against those who protest. They must be regarded as unpatriotic criminals who follow the imperialist instructions [directives] issued by the headquarters of the Catholic Church, by Vatican City.

During this phase, the masses will experience a psychological conflict because on the one hand, they will feel loyalty toward the Church and the Clergy, and, on the other hand, their patriotism will push them to support the People's Government. This conflict should be explored and studied with attention. If one acts precipitously without keeping in mind the acuteness of this psychological conflict, one risks isolating [alienating] the sympathy of these masses. If the bonds between the masses and the Church are very close, the principle of two steps forward and one step backward should be followed. In taking the step backward the People's government must state that it is defending religious freedom and that by the will of the masses, it is establishing reform committees in the associations so that the patriotic masses may express themselves more directly in the leadership of the affairs of the Church.

Let us be vigilant! The Party militants must direct the work of the reform committees. They must eliminate the reactionaries who will be found among the masses. For this job, these slogans must be followed: it is patriotic to adhere to the government and to observe the laws; disobedience is unpatriotic; the associations must profess their patriotism; the unpatriotic elements must be eliminated from the associations and judged as criminals by the masses; for it is the duty of every citizen to punish the criminals. The militants must turn the masses against the criminal elements. As soon as the masses have condemned the criminals and have eliminated them from the associations, they must be judged under the provisions of the laws of the People's government. At the same time, the associations will have to again profess their submission to the laws and make efforts to discover hidden counter-revolutionary activities among their members.

Though the reactionaries have been discovered, the psychological conflict among the masses must continue. It is important that the ecclesiastical authorities and the leaders of the Church should assure them that religion has become purer now that it has been freed from criminal and unpatriotic elements. Our militants who are members of these associations have the important task to cause the leaders of the Church to make these declarations. Of course, during this phase, other disagreements will arise. If one acts arbitrarily one will lose the control over the movement of the masses. The People's government must push in depth [to the utmost] the discussion of all disagreements. During these discussions, care should be taken to discover the counter-revolutionists who had previously gone unnoticed. During this phase, as in the one preceding it, the same slogans are called for: it is patriotic to observe the laws; disobedience is unpatriotic and criminal. The masses must also be informed of the results of conversations between the State and the Church, as well as of the patriotic renaissance of the religious masses in the process of taking the place of [divesting themselves of] decadent, imperialist, and unpatriotic sentiments. With the exception of spiritual affairs, every indication or expression of liaison with Vatican City will have to be spurned as being motivated by imperialist interests and supporting counter-revolutionary activities. The experience in the [our] brother [sister] countries proves that the Catholic Church has always sustained counter-revolutionary activities. Considering the universal scope of the Catholic Church, these experiences constitute irrefragable [irrefutable] proof of its conspiracy. During this phase, Vatican City may be expected to voice protests against our campaign. These protests must be utilized as further evidence of the conspiracy of the Church under the direction of Vatican City.

This leads us to the next phase in our attack; its object is the liaison which exists between the Church and Vatican City. It must be anticipated that in the course of the attack the clergy will react violently because it feels it has been struck at its point of support [foundations] and at the very source of its power. It [the Church] must be reminded that its protests against the attacks, of which it is the object because of its attachment to the Vatican, are unpatriotic and against the laws and the State. It must also be made to feel that what it incarnates is unpatriotic. It is the task of our militants to convince the masses that the individual may have his religion, without Vatican City directing the affairs of all Churches of the world. Our militants must also explain the principle of coexistence of patriotism and religion. Thus, those who follow the orders of the Vatican will be ousted from the masses, thus opening the road for the establishment of an independent Church.

A preparatory campaign must be made before a Church may be proclaimed independent. The clerics who cannot be persuaded to submit to the will of the government will be denounced before the masses. Their protests will be used to destroy their influence on the masses. The best tactic [to be followed] for this [purpose] will be to do a simple and anonymous job. Our militants must bring denunciations against these persons. History abounds in proof [examples] as to the possibility of legal action [action at law] against those who are opposed to a separation of the Church and the Vatican. During this phase all necessary arguments must be complied to convince the Catholic intellectuals that breaking with the Vatican is a step forward, not a step backward. The provisions of the law protecting all religions, and the history of the different protestant [protesting? — protest?] movements will help convince these intellectuals. At the same time, it will be the task of our militants to lead the Catholic associations into a comprehensive movement, requesting the People's government for authorization to establish an independent Church in order to remove from the Catholic associations any unpatriotic stain caused by elements still attached to the Vatican. The People's government will give the authorization, and the independent Church will be organized. It must be kept in mind that the break between the Catholic Church and the Vatican is of importance only for the theologians. The masses, in practicing their religion, are only weakly linked with the Vatican.

And now we have come to the last stage. The separation of Church and Vatican having been consummated, we can proceed to consecrating the leaders of the Church chosen by us. This will arouse the loud protest of the Vatican and major excommunication. It must be made clear that the struggle is carried on away from the faithful and in no way from within their midst [from without and not from within the group of believers]. The Catholic associations will continue to operate, and the masses will be encouraged to practice their religion in the new Church. If one acts with tact and wisdom [if tact and wisdom are applied], one will not destroy the liturgy and the masses will notice only slight differences in the new Church; the protests of the Vatican against the consecration of bishops will reach only the hierarchy of the Church, and the People's government will take charge of rejecting the complaints of the Vatican. Thus, the "old guard" of the Vatican will gradually be isolated. So isolated, action against it will become more and more legal; for it will feel a violent need for protest and playing the martyr. As a result of this attitude, it can only compromise itself by unpatriotic actions.

Though our struggle against the Catholic Church may be victorious, we must use [the force of] persuasion toward the rear-guard of the clergy. This moderate attitude will make the masses understand that the People's Government is truly anxious to guarantee freedom of religion to everyone. And, at the same time, the protestors are ranked with those who are opposed to the feelings of the people and the government.

Once the key posts of the clergy are in our hands and submitted to the People's Government, one will proceed to progressively eliminating from the liturgy those elements which are incompatible with the People's Government. The first changes will affect the sacraments and the prayers. Then, the masses will be protected against all pressure and all obligation to put in an appearance in the church, to practice religion, or to organize associations of whatever religious group.[2] We know full well that when the practice of religion becomes no more than an individual responsibility, it is slowly forgotten. New generations will follow the old, and religion will be no more than an episode of the past, worthy of being dealt with in the history [books] of the World Communist Movement.

Translated by ELIZABETH HANUNIAN,
Legislative Reference Service, Library of Congress.

[1]Explanatory note of the translator [from Chinese to Spanish to French].
[2][In Spanish:] "Then the masses will be protected against constraint and pressure to attend church, to practice religion, or to organize collective groups representing whatever religious sect."

TRANSLATION (Russian)

APPEAL

OF THE PARTICIPANTS OF THE ALL-UNION CONFERENCE OF THE RELATIVES OF PRISONERS OF THE CHURCH OF ECHB [EVANGELICAL CHRISTIAN BAPTISTS] IN THE U.S.S.R.

To all EChB, saints and faithful in Jesus Christ: Happiness and peace to you from God our Father and God Jesus Christ.

Beloved Brothers and Sisters, St. Paul, in his epistle to the Philippians wrote: "* * * my bonds in Christ are manifest in all the palace" and that "the things that happened unto me have fallen out rather unto the furtherance of the gospel."— (Phil. 1: 12-13.)

It happened to St. Paul in the first century, but today, it is happening with our relatives and ourselves, although it is now the 20th century.

We, the relatives of prisoners, also want that what happens to us may serve the furtherance of the work of God and, therefore, we want that the imprisonments of our relatives become known to all of you so that you may be participants in that body about which it is said: that it is "fitly joined together and compacted by that which every joint supplieth."—(Eph. 4: 16.)

Apostle Paul asked the servant of the Christ's Church, Timothy: "Be not thou ashamed of the testimony of our Lord, nor of me, his prisoner."—(II Tim. 1: 8.) "Remember my bonds", he asked the Church in his letter to the Colossians. —(Col. 4: 18.)

At this time, your own brothers and sisters beg of you: "Be not ashamed of us, remember our bonds."

We thank God for you, that, due to your serving Him, we, though persecuted by the world, are not left alone and, through you, God in his word, satisfies our needs. And we ask you that, in your prayers to God, you always remember your brothers and sisters in prisons.

How sad it is to read about the case Prophet Jeremiah—(Jer. 38: 15-13): The only man who remembered the bonds of the Prophet who was in a dungeon, was the heathen Ebed-melech, the Egyptian, but of the people of Israel for whom Prophet Jeremiah had shed tears—(Jer. 9: 1) and whom he wished all the best with all his heart, nobody remembered his sufferings in the dungeon. Today, the blood of Jesus Christ, our Lord, united us in one body and, therefore, if one member suffers, the whole body suffers; when one member is praised, the whole body is praised with him.

We wish to suffer jointly and to enjoy jointly the comforting of Christ, and all the Saints who constitute the Church of God and Christ!

Therefore, if there is someone else who is in a similar situation as we are, having brothers, husbands or sons imprisoned for the world of God, let us know about them and we shall notify the Church.

The Church, in its prayers, will convey the message to its Head, Jesus Christ, who will soon send his protection.

Our Lord is not indifferent to the sufferings of His Church, as the scripture says: "What toucheth you, toucheth the apple of His eye."

Therefore we shall not hide our sufferings from the Lord in the face of His Church. We shall say, with Paul the Apostle, that we, too, boast of our sorrows —(Rom. 5: 23). We also want to share with you the sorrows which we, the mothers bear, as our children were taken away from us.

Loving them and following the Word of God, that the "future generations to which children will be born" may know (Ps. 78: 4-7) and also having received a direct command of God (Heb. 6: 4), we brought up and educated our children according to God's teaching. For this, we were separated from our children.

Only you can fully conceive this sorrow, as you are the members of one living body of the Church of Christ, which is also threatened with such participation [in suffering].

We implore you, our brothers and sisters, in our Lord, Jesus Christ and in the love of the Spirit, to rise with us in your prayers to God for our relatives who are in prisons, listed in the information we are herewith enclosing as well as for us and our children.

God bless you!

Yours in Christ, brothers and sisters, relatives of prisoners for the Word of God.

At the direction of the All-Union Conference of relatives of the prisoners, EChB in the U.S.S.R.

February 23, 1964

1. GOVORUN (Smolensk)
2. IASTREBOVA (Kharkov)
3. RUDNEVA (Semipalatinsk).

Tortured For Christ

"Tortured For Christ" is the urgent plea of the abandoned Church behind the Iron Curtain. It is delivered to us by the most eloquent free voice, the Rev. Richard Wurmbrand, himself liberated from prison only in 1964. It is a two-fold message, for it is, on the one side, an urgent warning to the West that either Communism must be halted or the Free World will perish, and on the other a sublime epistle of love; the love of Christ for the communists offered in His Name by the very ones whom the Communists persecute.

Listen to Wurmbrand!

"Listen to Wurmbrand!" is the startling and unnerving detailed testimonies about the Christian Church and other tortured peoples and about his own prison experiences given at their invitation before U.S. Senators and Congressmen, the United States Senate Internal Subcommittee in 1966 and 1967, and before British Members of Parliament in July, 1967. In addition it contains a special prologue and epilogue by the author, including many of the latest facts regarding developments behind the Iron Curtain, and together with this the *only and most detailed series of vivid drawings of actual prison conditions and tortures ever to be published*. The drawings are by The Rev. Thomas Mails, himself a well known author and illustrator.

Also to be published in early 1968, by Coward McCann, CHRIST IN THE COMMUNIST PRISONS, which is the complete and profound Wurmbrand Story. This is a book which will easily rank with the finest biographies of our time!